BASEBALL NOW!

LaSalle Bank
THOME TICKER
499
K OUT THE SOX AT WWW.W
PITCH SPEED
90

BASEBALL NOW!

DAN BORTOLOTTI

A FIREFLY BOOK

Published by Firefly Books Ltd. 2008

First printing

Publisher Cataloging-in-Publication Data (U.S.)
Bortolotti, Dan.
    Baseball Now! / Dan Bortolotti.
[176] p. : col. ill. ; cm.
Includes index.
Summary: Features player profiles as well as up-to-date coverage of the 2007 regular season, playoffs and World Series.
ISBN-13: 978-1-55407-337-5 (pbk.)
ISBN-10: 1-55407-337-5 (pbk.)
1. Baseball. 2. Baseball players. 3. Major League Baseball.
I. Title.
796.357/092/2 dc22   GV865.A1.B678   2008

Library and Archives Canada Cataloguing in Publication
Bortolotti, Dan
    Baseball now! / Dan Bortolotti.
Includes index.
ISBN-13: 978-1-55407-337-5
ISBN-10: 1-55407-337-5
    1. Baseball--Biography. 2. Baseball. I. Title.
GV865.A1B67 2008   796.357092'2   C2007-904472-7

Published in the United States by
Firefly Books (U.S.) Inc.
P.O. Box 1338, Ellicott Station
Buffalo, New York 14205

Published in Canada by
Firefly Books Ltd.
66 Leek Crescent
Richmond Hill, Ontario L4B 1H1

Cover and interior design by Luna Design

Printed in Canada

The publisher gratefully acknowledges the financial support for our publishing program by the Government of Canada through the Book Publishing Industry Development Program.

For my dad, who first brought me to the ballpark, and for Jaimie and Erick, who brought me back

contents

Bud Selig likes to call this the golden era of baseball. Of course, Major League Baseball's commissioner has a vested interest in putting on a happy face, but the game truly is thriving as never before. For the fourth season in a row, MLB set a new attendance record in 2007, with almost 80 million fans buying peanuts and Cracker Jack. Meanwhile, in July of that year, NFL quarterback Michael Vick was being charged for running a dog-fighting ring and NBA referee Tim Donaghy was found to have gambled on games that he officiated. Perhaps it was not a coincidence that baseball's single-day attendance record was smashed on July 28, when 717,478 people took in a major-league game.

Five or six years ago, this unprecedented interest in baseball would have been hard to predict. Indeed, from the mid-1990s until well into the new millennium, the sport was in crisis. After the 1994 players' strike — which wiped out the postseason for the first time in history — fans stayed away in droves: attendance in 1993 had spiked at 70.2 million, and two years later it plummeted

by 30 percent. The power-hitting heroics of Mark McGwire and Sammy Sosa coaxed more fans through the turnstiles in 1998, but attendance declined again every season from 2000 to 2003 as it became clear that anabolic steroids were a main reason for the recent rash of home runs. The lowest point may have come in the second half of the 2002 season, when yet another players' strike seemed imminent.

What has reignited interest in baseball? For one, while the salary cap, the "competitive balance draft" and other schemes for leveling the playing field never came to pass, the problem of domination by big-money teams has lessened. While clubs in New York, Boston and Los Angeles continue to be successful, they are repeatedly challenged by small-market clubs in Oakland, St. Louis, Colorado, Arizona and Minnesota. America's national pastime is also increasingly international: the emergence of Japanese-born stars, especially, is enriching the game the way that European players revolutionized the National Hockey League in the early 1990s. Finally, baseball has made strides toward preventing the use

of banned substances. In addition to doing more rigorous testing, MLB unveiled a new policy in 2005 that includes a 50-game suspension for players who test positive for steroid use once, and a lifetime ban for three-time offenders.

Baseball still faces a number of challenges. Stratospheric salaries and rising ticket prices continue to alienate fans, and now that postseason games are all played at night, the youngest generation misses out on one of the best parts of October — unless they sneak a radio under the covers. The legacy of performance-enhancing drugs also remains: witness the lukewarm reaction to Barry Bonds' 756th home run on August 7, 2007. What should have been one of the greatest moments in the game's history was clouded by indifference, and even contempt. As Bonds approached Hank Aaron's hallowed mark, an ABC News/ESPN poll revealed that more than half of baseball fans hoped Bonds would fail to break the record, and only 58 percent believed he belongs in the Hall of Fame. Fortunately, many of those negative feelings were erased by another incredible performance the same day Bonds tied Aaron's record,

as Alex Rodriguez became the youngest player ever to reach 500 home runs. Only a career-ending injury will stop him from eventually eclipsing Bonds.

For the true fan the essence of baseball is not found in labor disputes, salary arbitration or drug policies. What keeps people coming to the ballpark in record numbers is the elegance of the game itself. Baseball is the thinking fan's sport: the rare game with no clock, where it truly ain't over until it's over. It is, as the cliché goes, a game of inches in which the finest line separates a two-out walk from an inning-ending strikeout, a dramatic stolen base from a rally-killing out, or a foul ball from a game-winning home run.

Above all, baseball is about the players. It is a team game, to be sure, but it is defined by one-on-one confrontations: pitcher and batter separated by 60 feet, six inches. Perhaps more than any other sport, it can humble the mighty and make a hero of yesterday's goat. This inaugural edition of *Baseball Now!* celebrates the best players in the game today: the athletes who have helped shape the golden era of the grand old game.

INTRODUCTION

Outstanding
OUTFIELDERS

jason
BAY

British Columbia is the center of the logging industry in Canada, but in Trail, BC, the only lumber that matters is the bat wielded by Jason Bay.

The town of Trail (population 8,000) has sent at least nine players to the National Hockey League, but it wasn't until 2004 that the Bay family put their hometown on the baseball map. Jason's sister Lauren was a pitcher for Canada's softball team in the Olympics that summer, while her big brother won Rookie of the Year honors in the National League.

Jason Bay made his debut with the San Diego Padres in May 2003, but in just his eighth at-bat he was plunked by a pitch and suffered a fractured right wrist. He was playing again in the minors by July, but was traded to Pittsburgh in August. He got into 27 games with the Pirates that year, the most memorable being the opener of a doubleheader at PNC Park, where Bay hit his first career grand slam off Cubs' ace Carlos Zambrano, and then added a two-run homer and a two-run double for a total of eight RBIs. It was a preview of what was to come in his first full season.

The 2004 campaign started late for Bay, as he had shoulder surgery in the offseason and didn't join the Pirates until May. He quickly made up for lost time, finishing the season with 26 home runs — a club record for rookies — and led all NL first-year players in homers, RBIs, slugging, total bases and extra-base hits. Bay's sophomore season was even better,

as he improved to .306 with 32 homers, while scoring 110 runs and driving in 102. He also demonstrated the good instincts that managers like to see in young ballplayers. With only average speed he swiped 21 bases while being caught only once, and his patience at the plate resulted in 95 walks, pushing his on-base percentage over .400. Those positive numbers put a silver lining on his 142 strikeouts.

On defense, Bay does a good job patroling the spacious left field in PNC Park, and makes very few errors, though he has been criticized for his lack of arm strength — *The Hardball Times* ranks him near the bottom of the NL in preventing runners from taking an extra base. While Bay insists that his right arm is healthy, the broken wrist and shoulder surgery he endured in 2003 may have left a permanent legacy.

As the 2006 All-Star Game approached, the Pirates cranked up the public relations machine on Bay's behalf. The Midsummer Classic was at PNC Park that year, so the Pirates were eager to see one of their own in the starting lineup.

$ 24.95
GATE 14
SECTION CLUB
SEAT A38
L1KB449
12JUNE08

CAREER HIGHLIGHTS

- only Pirate ever to combine a .300 average with 30 homers, 40 doubles, 100 runs, 100 RBIs and 20 stolen bases in the same season (2005)

- batted .455 for Team Canada in the 2006 World Baseball Classic, including going 2-for-3 in a victory over the US

- already ranks fourth in career home runs by a Canadian, trailing only Larry Walker, Matt Stairs and Jeff Heath

38 LEFT FIELD

Jason BAY

Bay helped his own case with a marvelous May, during which he hit 12 home runs, including going deep in six straight games. The campaign worked: Bay finished second in fan voting, trailing only Albert Pujols, and he started the game in right field and batting cleanup. He would go on to have another fine season in 2006, with 35 homers and 109 RBIs.

Unfortunately, the Pirates finished that year with a dismal 67–95 record, second last in the weakest division in baseball. During the offseason they acquired Adam LaRoche from the Atlanta Braves, hoping that another power hitter — the first baseman had 32 homers in 2006 — would form a one-two punch with Bay. Toss in defending NL batting champ Freddy Sanchez ahead of the two sluggers in the lineup, and it appeared as though the team might score some runs in 2007. That didn't work out — all three players performed below expectations and the Pirates finished in the basement. As the team retools for the future, they'll look to Jason Bay to lead the way.

carlos BELTRAN

Carlos Beltran and the Kansas City Royals are a classic illustration of why small-market teams are at such a disadvantage in Major League Baseball. When the 22-year-old Beltran earned a job as the Royals' everyday center fielder in 1999, he was flanked by Jermaine Dye and Johnny Damon in the most promising young outfield in the league. But by 2005, all three players were starring for teams with deeper pockets — Dye with White Sox, Damon with the Red Sox, and Beltran with the Mets.

Beltran was drafted by KC in 1995 and spent the majority of the next three years in the minors, where he taught himself to switch-hit like his idol, fellow Puerto Rican Bernie Williams. Beltran was a late-season call-up in 1998, and then surpassed all expectations in 1999 during his first full year with the Royals, batting .293 with 22 homers, 112 runs scored, 108 RBIs and 27 stolen bases. No rookie had scored 100 and driven in 100 since Fred Lynn in 1975. As a result, Beltran was the near-unanimous choice as the AL's Rookie of the Year.

His sophomore season was more difficult. By July he had only six home runs and was batting around .250 when he injured his knee. Then he was suspended by the Royals for refusing to report to the minors for a rehab assignment. He redeemed himself with three highly productive years, collecting at least 24 homers, 100 runs, 100 RBIs and a .500 slugging percentage each season from 2001 to 2003. Showing more discipline in 2003, he drew 72 walks to go along with his .307 average and placed ninth in the AL MVP voting.

By 2004 Beltran had emerged as one of the best all-around outfielders in the game, and everyone knew his days in Kansas City were numbered. His contract was up at the end of the year, and the cash-strapped Royals, headed for a last-place finish, knew they would be unable to woo him back. Beltran began the season at a good clip and was voted to the All-Star Team for the

first time, but on June 24 he was dealt to the Houston Astros. Three weeks later, he became the first player to play for the NL All-Star Team after being selected to the AL squad.

Beltran put on an incredible show during his brief stay in Houston. In just 90 games he belted 23 homers and added 28 steals, helping the Astros secure the wild card spot in the postseason. Facing the Atlanta Braves in the National League Division Series, Beltran went 3-for-3 with a home run in Game 1, homered again in Game 3, and then went 4-for-5 with two home runs and five RBIs to help win the deciding fifth match. Although the Astros lost to the St. Louis Cardinals in the NLCS, Beltran hit one out of the park in each of the first four games. His eight postseason home runs tied Barry Bonds' 2002 major-league record.

The Astros were obviously eager to re-sign Beltran when he became a free agent at the end of the season, but they were outbid by the New York Mets, who offered him a seven-year, $119-million deal. Beltran's

first season with the Mets in 2005 was disappointing, as his totals dropped to 16 home runs and 78 RBIs. The low point came in August when he collided with right fielder Mike Cameron as both dived for a shallow fly ball. Beltran suffered a concussion and cuts to his face, while Cameron fared even worse, missing the rest of the season with a broken nose and fractured cheekbones.

Beltran followed up that poor season with a big comeback. Playing healthy in 2006, he had career highs in home runs (41), RBIs (116), on-base percentage (.388) and slugging percentage (.594) to win his first Silver Slugger Award. His sure-handed play in center field — just two errors in 359 chances — also earned him his first Gold Glove.

After a strong start in 2007, Beltran was ice-cold until the stretch drive, and then he cranked it up several notches. He slugged .613 in August and September, including 14 home runs, finishing with 33 dingers, 112 RBIs and his second straight Gold Glove. Unfortunately for the center fielder, it wasn't enough to stop the Mets from imploding in the final week and finishing out of the postseason.

$ 24.95
GATE

SECTION 5
CLUB

SEAT K21

H3BG562
3JULY08

CAREER HIGHLIGHTS

- one of only six players to record three seasons with 100 runs, 100 RBIs and 30 stolen bases (he did so each year from 2001 to 2004)

- set record with home runs in five consecutive postseason games (2004)

- named to four straight All-Star Teams (2004–07)

15   CENTER FIELD

Carlos BELTRAN

carl
CRAWFORD

There has never been much for baseball fans to cheer about in Tampa Bay. In the Devil Rays' first ten seasons, they finished dead last in the American League East nine times. But at least the long-suffering souls who show up at Tropicana Field have the privilege of watching Carl Crawford, perhaps the most exciting player in the game.

Crawford was born in Houston in 1981 and raised by his mother in the Fifth Ward, a neighborhood rife with poverty, drugs and gangs. With the encouragement of his mom and his uncle Jack Crawford — who had played in the California Angels' system — young Carl stayed out of trouble by focusing on sports. In his senior year at Jefferson Davis High School he was an All-State quarterback and a star point guard on the basketball team while batting .563 on the diamond. He received scholarship offers from Nebraska (football) and UCLA (basketball), but decided to sign with the Devil Rays when they drafted him 52nd overall in 1999 and handed him a $1.2-million bonus.

Tampa Bay rushed the 20-year-old Crawford into the big leagues in July 2002, and in his first 21 games he smacked five triples, showing a glimpse of the hitter he would soon become. Crawford's performance earned him the full-time job as the D-Rays' left fielder and leadoff hitter for 2003, and he made his mark early. On Opening Day, Crawford hit a walk-off three-run homer with two outs in the ninth to overcome a 4–3 Red Sox lead.

CAREER HIGHLIGHTS

- one of 11 players to record 50 steals, 50 extra-base hits and 100 runs in the same season (2004)

- second player in the postwar era to have consecutive seasons of 15 triples and 15 homers (2005–06)

- improved his average and home run totals for five straight seasons (2002–06), joining Rogers Hornsby as the only players to accomplish that feat

13 LEFT FIELD

Carl CRAWFORD

While he showed some pop in his bat, it was Crawford's blazing speed that made him so exciting to watch. In his first full season he led the AL with 55 stolen bases, and then bested that total the following year with a team-record 59 thefts. In 2004, he also hit a major-league-high 19 triples and was the toughest player to double up — he grounded into just two DPs in 626 at-bats. He was rewarded for his hard work in July when Joe Torre selected him to play in the All-Star Game at Minute Maid Field in Houston, a short drive from where Crawford grew up. Tampa Bay rewarded him again after the season with a big contract to keep him a Ray until at least 2008.

Concerned about his reluctance to walk and his relatively low on-base percentage, manager Lou Piniella tried Crawford in the number-two and number-three spots in 2005, and he responded with a career-high 15 homers and 81 RBIs. The speedster was finally beginning to find his power stroke consistently, and after he had again led the league with 15 triples,

observers started to wonder whether Crawford might one day become the fifth player (after Frank Schulte, Willie Mays, Curtis Granderson and Jimmy Rollins) to collect 20 doubles, 20 triples, 20 homers and 20 steals in the same season.

Crawford had a red-hot first half in 2006, batting .323 with 13 homers and 32 steals at the break. His biggest game came on May 24 against the Toronto Blue Jays, as he went 5-for-5 with a homer, four stolen bases and five runs scored. On July 5 against Boston, Crawford "stole for the cycle," swiping second, third and home to reach 200 career steals, one of just eight players to do so before age 25. By the end of the season his average stood at .305, and he had upped his personal best in homers to 18, while topping the AL in both three-base hits (16) and stolen bases (58).

There seems to be no stopping Carl Crawford. He was an All-Star again in 2007, and while he hit just nine triples and 11 homers, he smacked 37 doubles, upped his average for the sixth straight year (finishing with a career-high .315) and led the AL for the fourth time with 50 steals. Few players have matched Crawford's accomplishments at the plate and on the base paths at such a young age. He is on pace to reach 1,000 hits, 100 triples and 300 steals before age 28. The only other player to do that in the modern era? Just a guy named Ty Cobb.

ken
GRIFFEY JR.

On June 22, 2007, Ken Griffey Jr. made a triumphant and unlikely return to Seattle. Just four years earlier, after the Reds' center fielder suffered an injury that ended his 2003 season, a *Sports Illustrated* columnist remarked on "how quickly and fully Griffey went from being baseball's poster child to being plainly irrelevant." Now here he was returning to the city where he was considered the savior of baseball. The Seattle faithful welcomed Junior with a three-minute standing ovation and a video tribute showcasing that sweet swing, those leaping catches, and most of all, that big Ken Griffey smile. Junior responded with a hit in his first at-bat that night, and in the series finale he hit two balls right out of Safeco Field, the place they call "The House That Griffey Built."

When the 19-year-old won a spot in the Seattle lineup in 1989, the Mariners were one of the worst teams in baseball, having never finished above .500 since joining the AL a dozen years earlier. Now the patient fans had a reason to come to the ballpark — and right on cue, the teenaged Griffey homered on the first pitch of his first at-bat in the old Kingdome. In his sophomore season, Junior became the youngest player to start an All-Star Game in 45 years, and the youngest outfielder to win a Gold Glove, all while batting .300 with 22 homers.

The once-hopeless Mariners got their first taste of the postseason in 1995. Griffey had missed much of the season after breaking his wrist making a spectacular diving catch, but when he returned in August the Mariners came alive, first erasing a 13-game deficit to tie

$ 24.95
GATE 17
SECTION FIELD
SEAT NN03
R8TE638
29MAY08

CAREER HIGHLIGHTS

- named to MLB's All-Century Team in 1999, by far the youngest member at 29 years old

- won 10 consecutive Gold Gloves in center field (1990–99)

- ranks sixth on the all-time home run list with 593

3   RIGHT FIELD

Ken GRIFFEY JR.

the California Angels, then defeating them in a one-game playoff to win their first division title. After losing two of the first three matches in the best-of-five ALDS against the Yankees, Griffey hit a game-tying homer (his fourth of the series) in Game 4, and homered again in Game 5 to help the Mariners rally back from a 4–2 deficit. Then, in the bottom of the 11th with Griffey on first, Edgar Martinez smacked a double into the left field corner and Junior raced all the way home to score the winning run and clinch the series.

Junior's biggest season came in 1997, when he notched a record 32 homers before the break and received over six million All-Star votes, another record. He finished with 56 home runs, 147 RBIs, his eighth Gold Glove and 28 out of 28 first-place votes for the American League MVP. Amazingly, he had almost the exact same power totals again the following year — 56 homers and 146 RBIs — joining Babe Ruth and Lou Gehrig as the only players to drive in 140-plus runs in three straight seasons. He accomplished these feats drug-free in an era when other power hitters were juicing their swings with performance-enhancing substances.

Before the 2000 season, Griffey made it known that he wanted to be dealt to Cincinnati. It was where he

grew up, where his dad, Ken Griffey Sr., had played his best years, and where his parents still lived. The Reds had barely missed the playoffs in 1999 and were hoping Griffey would vault them into the postseason. He did not. In his first season in the National League, he collected 40 homers (including the 400th of his career) and 118 RBIs, but the Reds finished 10 games back.

Then came the injuries: seven stints on the DL between 2001 and 2004. Even his comeback season in 2005 (when he hit .301 with 35 homers) was cut short after he sprained his foot in early September. He suffered a knee injury and a broken toe in 2006, and in the offseason, while playing with his children, he broke his hand. He was 37 years old and the Reds were facing another dreadful season, yet no one was talking about retirement. He lost his job in center, moving to right field for the first time in his career, but despite the obstacles Griffey went on to play 144 games for the first time since 2000, adding another 30 home runs to edge closer to the 600 mark.

Had Griffey not been so crippled by injuries, he would have taken a run at Hank Aaron's 755 career homers before Barry Bonds did. Had he broken the record, no one could have argued it was tainted.

vladimir
GUERRERO

If a ballplayer wanted to thrive in obscurity, the place to accomplish that was Montreal during its final years in the National League. During his five full seasons in right field for the Expos, Vladimir Guerrero batted a combined .325 and averaged 39 home runs and 117 RBIs, yet he went mostly unnoticed. In 2000, Guerrero hit .345 with 44 homers, 123 RBIs and a career-high slugging percentage of .664, yet finished sixth in the MVP voting. Things changed only after he signed with the Anaheim Angels before the 2004 season. That year he put up numbers that were merely normal for him — .337, 39 homers, 126 RBIs — but this time he did so on a division winner in California and won MVP honors by a landslide.

Guerrero, born in the Dominican Republic in 1976, tore up the Expos' minor-league system as a teenager. He was a September call-up at age 20 and promised to be the best rookie in the NL in 1997, but injuries permitted him to play only 90 games (he still batted .302 with 11 home runs). Over the next few seasons, however, he joined the ranks of the greatest young sluggers of all-time, batting over .300 with at least 30 homers and 100 RBIs each year from 1998 to 2000. Only a trio of players had achieved that feat three times before the age of 25: Ted Williams, Jimmie Foxx and Joe DiMaggio. (Albert Pujols would later join the group.) Guerrero reached those benchmarks again at ages 25 and 26 before spending 40 games on the disabled list in 2003.

Guerrero is not your stereotypical slugger. He doesn't whiff very often, and in several seasons he has collected more walks than strikeouts. Looking at those statistics, one might think Guerrero doesn't swing at bad pitches, but the truth is he'll flail at anything from his shoe tops to his eyes — and hit it hard. In Montreal, he once tallied a single on a ball that bounced before the plate, and in the 2006 All-Star Game he homered on a pitch at shoulder level.

After his years of excellence on lousy teams, Guerrero finally got a chance to play on a contender when he signed as a free agent with Anaheim. The Angels trailed Oakland in the AL West by three games in the final week of 2004, but rallied to win the division, thanks in part to Guerrero's performance in those seven games: 15-for-28 (.536) with six home runs and 11 RBIs. The charmed Red Sox swept the Angels in the ALDS that year, and Guerrero managed just two hits in 12 at-bats, but he made them count: a two-run single in Game 2, and a game-tying grand slam in the final match.

With his big bat and his bigger smile, Guerrero soon became a fan favorite in Anaheim, with its many Spanish-speaking fans. He is a quiet but charismatic family man who is active in the community, setting up, among other things, programs such as "Vlad's Pad," a block of tickets he donates to youth groups and charities for every home game.

Guerrero won over even more fans during the next two seasons with the Angels as he put up great numbers: he hit .317 with 32 home runs and 108 RBIs in 2005, and .329 with 33 homers and 116 RBIs in 2006. Indeed, Guerrero's play has been so remarkably consistent that he has never had what you could call a career year. He has finished no higher than third in his league in average, no higher than fourth in home runs or RBIs, and never better than fifth in slugging. Yet most managers would prefer Guerrero's kind of steady production to a couple of great seasons amid a decade of mediocrity.

Ironically, Guerrero's lowest power numbers came in 2007, the year he won the Home Run Derby at the All-Star Game. Although he pounded 17 balls into the stands during the derby on July 9, he went homerless from June 24 until August 2, the longest drought of his career, and finished with 27. (He still batted his usual .325 and drove in 125 runs.) Vlad also continued his pattern of poor performances in the postseason in 2007, collecting two singles in 10 at-bats as the Angels were again swept by the Red Sox. In his career, Guerrero owns a .183 average with one extra-base hit in 60 playoff games.

$ 24.95

GATE 4

SECTION UPPER

SEAT BB26

N6SS474

23JULY08

CAREER HIGHLIGHTS

- has batted over .300 for 11 seasons (1997–07), currently the longest streak in the majors

- one of five players to hit .300 with 30 homers and 100 RBIs in five straight seasons

- narrowly missed joining the 40–40 club in 2002 when he stole a career-high 40 bases and hit 39 home runs

27

RIGHT FIELD

Vladimir GUERRERO

matt HOLLIDAY

No one can accuse Matt Holliday of not paying his dues. Growing up in Stillwater, Oklahoma, Holliday was a superb athlete who worked out hard and paid strict attention to his diet. A solid six-foot-four in his senior year of high school, he excelled in baseball, basketball and football, and by the time he reached Oklahoma State University — where his father, Tom, was the baseball coach — it looked like Matt was headed for stardom as an NFL quarterback. Baseball scouts seemed to think so, too, and he was passed over again and again in the 1998 draft until the Colorado Rockies finally grabbed him in the seventh round.

Holliday agreed to sign, but he certainly wasn't fast-tracked into the majors. Though he was a hard worker with a commitment that coaches dream about, he was an inconsistent performer, and he toiled away in the Rockies' minor-league system for more than six years. Other than his first year at the lowly Rookie level, he never hit higher than .276 and averaged 11 homers a season. During Holliday's first four years in the minors, which he played no higher than Class-A, it looked as if he might never live up to his promise.

In the summer of 2001, the Rockies offered Holliday a big-league contract and guaranteed him $700,000 annually for six years — ensuring that he wouldn't return to the gridiron — but he still played all of 2002 and 2003 in Double-A. At 24 years old, Holliday began the 2004 season in Triple-A, but after just six games he

was called up when injuries left two gaping holes in the Rockies' outfield. Holliday made his MLB debut in left field on April 13 and has never looked back.

After facing minor-league hurlers for so many years, Holliday's nerves got the best of him in his first few games, and he started his career by going 0-for-7. But once the butterflies were gone he went on a tear, smacking 12 hits in his next 19 at-bats, including three doubles and a couple of home runs. Holliday was the second-best rookie left fielder in the NL that season — the Pirates' Jason Bay stole the show — and he made himself a fixture in the starting lineup with a .290 average, 31 doubles and 14 homers in just 400 at-bats.

Given his spotty minor-league record, it was easy to see Holliday's 2004 season as a fluke, and that speculation continued when he started slowly in 2005. Things got worse after he suffered a broken finger that landed him on the DL for almost six weeks. Upon returning in late July, however, he batted .323 the rest of the way, popping 15 home runs. In the month of September he piled up a league-leading 32 RBIs, eight of them coming in one game.

Holliday's long-awaited breakout season came in 2006, when he established himself as one of the best-hitting corner outfielders in the game. Finally showcasing his latent power, Holliday was second in the NL in extra-base hits (84) and fifth-best in slugging (.586). He batted .326 and belted 34 home runs to go along with 114 RBIs and 119 runs scored, good enough for his first Silver Slugger Award. While he no doubt benefits from the hitter-friendly dimensions of Coors Field, a couple of tape-measure homers that season proved that his power is genuine: his longest drive at home travelled an estimated 478 feet, and he launched another in Los Angeles that almost exited Dodger Stadium.

In 2007 the left fielder's performance was even more outstanding, and as the Rockies built a head of steam during the stretch drive, Holliday turned into a monster. In mid-September, he mashed 11 homers and drove in 21 runs in 12 games. In the last dozen games on the regular schedule he batted .457 as Colorado went 11–1 to force a one-game playoff against the Padres. In that thrilling tiebreaker, Holliday ripped a game-tying triple off Trevor Hoffman in the 13th inning and then raced home to score the winning run with a dramatic head-first slide that almost knocked him out. He then led his club to its first World Series appearance with five homers and 10 RBIs in 11 postseason games.

Holliday's season had MVP written all over it: he won the batting title (.340) and led the league with 216 hits, 50 doubles, 92 extra-base hits, 386 total bases and 137 RBIs. Yet the baseball writers passed him over in favor of the Phillies' charismatic Jimmy Rollins, who had a career year in 2007. Holliday, who is used to working hard and waiting patiently for success, will no doubt be in contention for the league's top prize for years to come.

torii HUNTER

LOS ANGELES ANGELS ◆ AL West

It wasn't easy to patrol center field in Minnesota — and not only because balls sometimes strike the Metrodome's Teflon roof, or because the wall in right-center looks and behaves like a giant garbage bag. The toughest part was living with the ghost of Kirby Puckett, who was the face of the Twins from 1984 until he was forced to retire due to glaucoma after the 1995 season. But for nine years Torii Hunter did it with equal measures of skill and class.

Born into poverty in Pine Bluff, Arkansas, Hunter traveled a difficult road to the big leagues. His father was a crack addict, and Torii remembers days with no electricity, and having to hide when bill collectors knocked on the door. His biggest motivation for getting to the majors was the promise of earning enough money to help his family. After achieving stardom, he bought homes for several family members and put his younger brothers through school.

Hunter was drafted in the first round by Minnesota in 1993. He struggled with the bat in the minors but established himself as a magnificent center fielder — during one game in Double-A, he ran right through the plywood fence to catch a would-be home run. He played all of 1999 with the big club, even hitting his first grand slam, but then spent half of 2000 in Triple-A and wondered whether he'd ever make it as a full-time major leaguer.

The answer came in 2001. While he continued his free-swinging habits, drawing just 29 walks and striking out 125 times, Hunter led the Twins with 27 home runs and was second with 92 RBIs. He was also dazzling in the outfield, making an incredible 460 putouts (still a career high) while committing just four errors and gunning down 14 runners. That performance won him his first Gold Glove and guaranteed him a permanent place on the roster. The Twins also turned a corner that year: they had finished no higher than fourth in the AL Central in the previous eight seasons, but now found themselves in first place at the break. Though they faltered down the stretch, they became bona fide contenders who would go on to win their division in four of the next five campaigns. In the post-Puckett era, the revitalized Twins and their fans looked to Torii Hunter to be the new face of the franchise, and he didn't let them down. It helped that Hunter is, in the words of one *Sports Illustrated* writer, "one of the most gregarious, fun-loving, easy-goingest players in baseball."

When Ron Gardenhire took over as the Twins' manager in 2002, Hunter had another great year. He batted .371 in April and stayed hot enough to be voted to the All-Star Team, the first time a Twin had started the Midsummer Classic since Puckett did so in 1995. He wasted no time staking out his territory: in the first inning, Barry Bonds drove a blast to center field that was headed over the wall until Hunter, timing his jump perfectly, leaped and pulled it back.

Hunter went on to slug 29 homers and 37 doubles in 2002 as the Twins finished first and defeated the Oakland A's in the American League Division Series before getting ousted by the Anaheim Angels. He posted similar numbers in 2003 and 2004, and both seasons ended the same way for the Twins: a first-place finish in the AL Central followed by an early exit from the playoffs at the hands of the powerhouse Yankees.

A broken ankle in July 2005 forced Hunter to miss almost half the season. Even still, his performance was good enough to win his fifth straight Gold Glove. Healthy again in 2006, Hunter had a career-high 31 homers to help earn the Twins another trip to the postseason. This time his glove failed him, however. After the Twins lost the opener of the ALDS to the A's, Game 2 was tied 2–2 in the seventh. With a man on, Oakland's Mark Kotsay hit a liner to right center that Hunter dove for and missed. The ball rolled to the wall and Kotsay roared around the bases with an inside-the-park home run. Two days later, the A's completed the sweep.

The Twins decided to exercise their option on Hunter for 2007 and he had another All-Star season, with 27 home runs and career highs in doubles (45) and RBIs (107). After becoming a free agent at the end of the year, he signed five-year deal with the Los Angeles Angels. With his golden glove flanked by Garrett Anderson and Vladimir Guerrero, Hunter will be at the center of one heavenly trio of Angels in the outfield.

$ 24.95

GATE 22

SECTION CLUB

SEAT J27

T4SC367   12JULY08

CAREER HIGHLIGHTS

- won seven consecutive Gold Gloves in center field (2001–07)
- has a career .300 average and a .538 slugging percentage in five postseason series
- collected at least 20 homers and 20 steals three times (2002, 2004, 2005)

48   CENTER FIELD

Torii **HUNTER**

andruw JONES

LOS ANGELES DODGERS ◆ NL West

Some of baseball's best prospects don't pan out until their mid-20s. Others, of course, don't ever live up to what the scouts saw in them. Then there's Andruw Jones, who burst onto the major-league stage in 1996 at the tender age of 19. While he hasn't quite lived up to all the hype — he had drawn comparisons with Ken Griffey Jr. and even Willie Mays — he has remained one of the game's top outfielders ever since.

Jones was born on the Caribbean island of Curacao, part of the Netherlands Antilles and hardly a baseball hot spot, and he signed with the Atlanta Braves when he was just 16. In 1995 Jones put up big numbers in Class-A, collecting 25 homers, 100 RBIs, 104 runs and 56 steals. He was quickly being called the best minor-league player on the planet.

The next year, Jones was in the minors barely long enough to get his uniform dirty. He started in Class-A, then jumped to Double-A in mid-June and to Triple-A in July. By August the Braves had called him up to the Show, and in his second game — aged 19 years, four months — he tripled and homered, becoming the youngest National Leaguer to go yard in more than 30 years. But it was in the 1996 World Series that Jones made history. Having already homered in his final at-bat of the NLCS, Jones stepped to the plate in Game 1 of the Series and launched one over the left-field wall at Yankee Stadium. In his next at-bat, he did it again. Only Reggie Jackson had ever

homered in three straight postseason at-bats — not bad company for a teenager.

The funny thing about Andruw Jones' amazing debut was that he wasn't touted as a home run hitter. In fact, even two seasons later, when the Braves made him their everyday center fielder, he began the year batting eighth. Where he truly excelled was on defense. During his first five seasons in center, dozens of extra-base hits died in Jones' glove as he recorded more than 400 putouts annually — including a staggering 493 in 1999 — and started a streak of 10 consecutive Gold Gloves. He has also led all major-league outfielders in assists during the last decade. In recent years, however, his range has been shrinking, and Jones' critics argue that his reputation as the best center fielder in the league is no longer deserved.

But while he may have lost a step in the outfield, Jones has become a masher at the plate. After averaging just over 30 home runs during his first eight seasons, he hit a league-leading 51 in 2005 to set a Braves record — and this is a franchise where lineup cards have included Hank Aaron, Eddie Matthews and Dale Murphy. He

followed that up with 41 long balls in 2006 to become the first Atlanta player with back-to-back 40-homer seasons. His career batting average is a mere .263 and he whiffs an average of 125 times a year, though he walks enough to post a decent on-base percentage, and scores close to a hundred runs a season. As well, Jones can be counted on to be out there every day: he has played at least 153 games in every campaign since 1997 to lead the major leagues in appearances over the last decade.

One thing Andruw Jones was unable to do in Atlanta was win a World Series, despite 10 consecutive division titles and two NL pennants. (After his storied performance in the 1996 Fall Classic, he went 1-for-13 in the 1999 rematch against the Yankees.) When Jones' contract expired in 2007, the Braves announced that they would not try to re-sign him, a decision made easier by his .222 average, .311 OBP and 26 home runs, half his total of two years earlier. In December, Jones signed a two-year deal with the Los Angeles Dodgers, a team in dire need of a power hitter. Despite his off-year, Jones no doubt has a lot of gas left in the tank. He patroled center field in Atlanta for so long that it's easy to forget he's barely 30 years old.

$ 24.95
GATE 15
SECTION UPPER
SEAT BB65
A3UK112
9SEPT08

CAREER HIGHLIGHTS

- won 10 Gold Gloves in center field, a feat topped only by Willie Mays (12)
- became the fourth-youngest player (28 years and 52 days old) to reach 300 homers (2006)
- collected his 1,500th hit and 1,000th RBI in 2006

25 CENTER FIELD

Andruw JONES

carlos LEE

After six years with the Chicago White Sox, Carlos Lee had worn out his welcome by the end of 2004 — or at least he had made the fatal mistake of running afoul of new manager Ozzie Guillen.

Under former White Sox field boss Jerry Manuel, Lee put together three seasons with at least 24 homers and 80 RBIs. In 2000, he was part of a quintet of sluggers (joining Frank Thomas, Magglio Ordonez, Jose Valentin and Paul Konerko) that hit 20-plus home runs each and powered the team to 95 wins and a division title. Lee had his best season with the Sox in 2003, collecting 31 dingers and driving in 113 runs. But the big left fielder (six-foot-two, 240 pounds) has long had a reputation for dogging it on the base paths, and the hot-headed Guillen has zero patience for players who give less than an all-out effort. Although Lee batted .305 in 2004 and matched his career high of 31 home runs — he even established a team record with a 28-game hit streak — the White Sox traded him to the Milwaukee Brewers at the conclusion of the season.

Lee thrived with his new National League team. He broke a Brewers club mark by driving in 76 runs in the first half — a feat that earned him a trip to his first All-Star Game — and though his average dropped to .265, he finished the season with personal bests in home runs (32) and RBIs (114), winning his first Silver Slugger Award. (Meanwhile, his former team, despite also losing Ordonez to free agency, won the World Series in 2005.)

Lee had another torrid first half the following year, pounding 26 home runs before the break in 2006. But the Brewers were unable to convince him to agree to a contract extension, and on July 28 they traded him to the Texas Rangers. In 59 games, he batted .322 with 19 doubles and nine homers, and during one stretch in August and September he reached safely in 32 straight games. He wound up batting a combined .300 with 37 homers, 116 RBIs, 75 extra-base hits and even swiped 19 bases, just missing membership in the 20–20 club.

While Lee may not win awards for his hustle, he has worked hard during his career to plug some gaps in his game. In his early years he struck out at least twice as often as he walked, but he has since greatly improved that ratio. In 2007 Lee whiffed about once in every 10 at-bats, an excellent rate for a hitter with such power. He has also focused on improving his defense. After committing a league-high eight errors in left field in 2001, and then seven more in 2003, he asked for extra coaching on his fly-catching skills, and in 2004 he was the only outfielder in the majors who played the whole season without a single miscue.

Carlos Lee became one of the most sought-after free agents at the end of the 2006 season. While he wouldn't stay in Arlington with the Rangers, he did settle in Texas, signing a six-year contract with the Houston Astros. Lee seems like a good fit in the Lone Star State: he breeds cattle in Agualduce, Panama, where he was born, and also owns a ranch outside Houston. While with the White Sox, Lee picked up the nickname El Caballo ("The Horse"), and his new cadre of fans at Minute Maid Park call themselves El Caballitos and ride stick ponies to cheer on the team's slugger. He went some way toward winning over the Houston faithful just nine games into the 2007 season, when he blasted three homers — including a grand slam — against the Phillies in a 9–6 win.

The Astros fell to 73–89 in 2007 and ranked near the bottom of the league in both pitching and runs scored. Lee was one of the bright spots, however, as he made his third straight All-Star appearance and led the Astros with 190 hits, 43 doubles and 119 RBIs while batting .303 with 32 home runs. After taking a while to feel at home outside Chicago, El Caballo has finally found a hitching post.

CAREER HIGHLIGHTS

- only player other than Alex Rodriguez to tally at least 150 homers, 550 RBIs and 70 stolen bases between 2003 and 2007

- named to the NL All-Star Team in three consecutive seasons (2005–07)

- recorded five straight 30-homer seasons (2003–07) while playing with four different teams

45 LEFT FIELD

Carlos LEE

$ 24.95
GATE **47**
SECTION **FIELD**
SEAT **K49**
L8KM490
9MAY08

magglio ORDONEZ

30

When the Detroit Tigers signed Magglio Ordonez as a free agent in February 2005, they included an escape clause. The slugging right fielder had strung together five magnificent seasons for the Chicago White Sox from 1999 to 2003, but his 2004 campaign lasted only 52 games because of a knee injury. So the Tigers offered Ordonez $75 million over five years — their biggest free-agent signing to date — but to make it clear they would not be buying damaged goods, they included a condition that would allow the team to take back Ordonez's $6 million signing bonus and cancel the deal if their new outfielder spent more than 25 days on the disabled list because of his wonky knee.

Ordonez was born in Caracas, Venezuela, and signed with the White Sox in 1991, when he was 17. He joined the big club at the end of the 1997 season and immediately became their everyday right fielder. The team's shortstop that year was Ozzie Guillen, a fellow Venezuelan who would go on to manage the club eight years later. Ordonez's breakout season came in 1999, when he batted .301 with 30 homers and 117 RBIs. He went on to have four more outstanding years in Chicago, during which he averaged 32 homers and slammed 40 or more doubles in three straight seasons, the first White Sox player ever to do so. But when Guillen took over in 2004, he made no secret that he wanted Ordonez gone. The two had never gotten along — they would later describe one another as "enemies" — and the outfielder ended up in Detroit before the 2005 season.

Some baseball insiders criticized the Tigers for spending such a huge sum on an injured player who looked to be past his prime. "It doesn't get much worse than this," said *The Hardball Times*. "We can state unequivocally that the Tigers have done something terrible." As it turned out, Ordonez's knee was fine. Unfortunately, just three games into his first season with Detroit, he suffered a sports hernia and didn't play again until July. He got off to a slow start, but soon showed the Tigers he was worthy of their faith by batting .343 in July and .323 in August. But it was the White Sox who had the last laugh in 2005: Ordonez's former team swept the Houston Astros in the Fall Classic, and his replacement in right field, Jermaine Dye, was World Series MVP.

The tables turned the following season. A healthy Ordonez hit 24 homers and posted his first 100-RBI year since 2002, helping the Tigers win 95 games and the AL wild card race. What Detroit fans will remember most about 2006 is what he did in the final game of the American League Championship Series against Oakland. Having already homered to tie the game in the sixth, Ordonez came to bat against Athletics' closer Huston Street in the bottom of the ninth. With two out, two on and the score knotted at threes, he took a 1–0 fastball and launched a rainbow shot over the left-field wall to send the Tigers to their first World Series since 1984.

Clearly comfortable in Detroit as he entered his third season as a Tiger, Ordonez had a career year in 2007. In late June he was batting .383, and with 35 two-baggers at the All-Star break, he looked like he might become the first player since 1936 to collect 60 doubles in a season (he wound up with a league-high 54). As the Tigers battled for a spot in the playoffs, Ordonez hit .393 with 31 RBIs in August — including two homers in one inning on August 12 — and finished with MVP-caliber numbers. He won the batting title with a .363 average, the highest by a Tiger since Hall of Fame second baseman Charlie Gehringer hit .371 way back in 1937. He added 28 home runs and a career-high 139 RBIs, second only to Alex Rodriguez. Indeed, it was only A-Rod's phenomenal performance in 2007 that prevented Ordonez from copping the league's top award: he received two first-place votes and finished a distant second.

Perhaps the most encouraging thing about Ordonez's magnificent season was that he stayed healthy and played 157 games. One would think that the Tigers have forgotten all about the escape clause in his contract.

$ 24.95
GATE 56
SECTION CLUB
SEAT A21
C5KJ477
4AUG08

CAREER HIGHLIGHTS

- first AL player to bat .300 with 40 doubles, 30 homers, 100 RBIs and 25 stolen bases in the same season (2001)

- was one homer and one RBI short (in 2003) of posting five straight seasons of with a .300 average, 30-plus home runs and 100-plus RBIs

- named to the AL All Star Team six times (1999–01, 2003, 2006–07)

30 RIGHT FIELD

Magglio ORDONEZ

manny
RAMIREZ

Manny Ramirez constantly surprises and frustrates Red Sox fans with his actions — whether it's failing to run out ground balls, missing 10 or 20 games a season due to mysterious ailments, or regularly discussing his desire to be traded. But the Fenway faithful have learned to accept it as "Manny being Manny." Sure, his uniform is two sizes too large and his dreadlocks trail down from the dirtiest batting helmet in baseball history, but Ramirez is too great a hitter to be remembered as just another colorful character.

Ramirez was born in Santo Domingo, Dominican Republic, in 1972, and moved to the Washington Heights neighborhood of Manhattan when he was 13. He wasn't a Yankees fan as a teenager, however; Manny cheered for the Toronto Blue Jays, who in the 1980s were one of the first teams to recruit players from his native country. He attended George Washington High School — the alma mater of the legendary Rod Carew — where scouts quickly recognized him as one of the hottest prospects in the country. The Cleveland Indians drafted Ramirez in the first round in 1991, and he made his debut with the club two years later.

In 1995 Ramirez moved into the ranks of the finest hitters in the league, socking 31 homers and driving in 107 runs to lead the Indians to the World Series. His first Fall Classic was disappointing, however — not only did Ramirez hit just .222, he showcased some of the maddening behaviour that would become his trademark. In the eighth inning of Game 2, with Jim Thome at the plate and his team trailing by a run, Ramirez was caught napping at first where he was promptly picked off. The Indians lost the game, and eventually the series. Two Octobers later, he batted .154 as the Indians lost the 1997 World Series to the Florida Marlins.

Though his head wasn't always in the game, Ramirez posted big numbers in 1998 (.294, 45 homers, 145 RBIs) and again in 1999, when he collected an

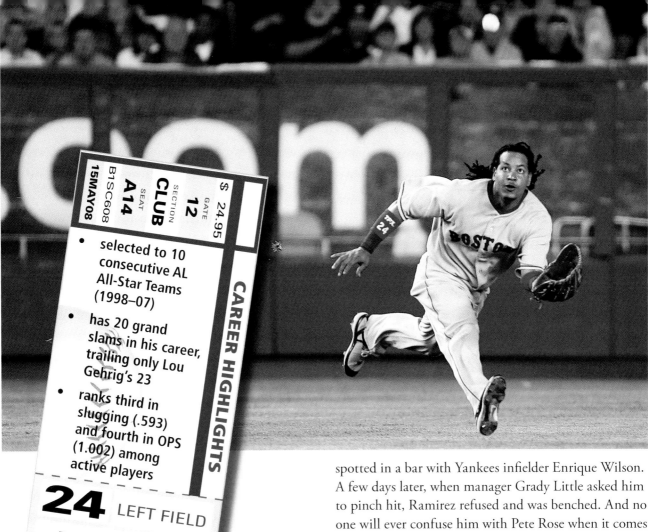

$ 24.95

GATE
12

SECTION
CLUB

SEAT
A14

B1SC608
15MAY08

CAREER HIGHLIGHTS

- selected to 10 consecutive AL All-Star Teams (1998–07)

- has 20 grand slams in his career, trailing only Lou Gehrig's 23

- ranks third in slugging (.593) and fourth in OPS (1.002) among active players

24 LEFT FIELD

Manny RAMIREZ

amazing 165 RBIs — the highest one-season total since 1938 — despite missing 15 games.

Manny became a free agent in 1999 and signed a $160-million contract with the Boston Red Sox that December. The Bosox moved him from right to left field, in front of Fenway Park's Green Monster, and he continued to pound the ball. In his first four seasons with his new team he averaged 38 homers and 116 RBIs and won the batting title in 2002 (.349). During Boston's magical playoff run in 2004 — when they reeled off eight straight wins for their first championship since 1918 — Ramirez exorcised his postseason demons. He was 5-for-13 (.385) with seven RBIs against the Angels in the American League Division Series and followed that up with a 9-for-30 (.300) clip against Yankee pitchers in the ALCS. He topped it all off by batting .412 and taking MVP honors in the World Series sweep over the Cardinals.

Through it all, however, Manny was still Manny. In August of 2003 he complained of illness and sat out a crucial series against New York, during which he was

spotted in a bar with Yankees infielder Enrique Wilson. A few days later, when manager Grady Little asked him to pinch hit, Ramirez refused and was benched. And no one will ever confuse him with Pete Rose when it comes to hustling on the base paths: twice during the 2005 stretch drive, Manny failed to run out ground balls that resulted in key outs, costing his team a win both times.

Ramirez battled his usual array of day-to-day injuries in 2007 and sat out more than 30 games, compiling some of the lowest power numbers of his career: 20 home runs, 88 RBIs and a .493 slugging percentage. But he was vintage Manny in the postseason: he blasted a walk-off three-run homer off Francisco Rodriguez with two outs in the ninth inning to beat the Angels in Game 2 of the ALDS, raising his arms and admiring it as the ball disappeared over the Green Monster. Facing his former team in the Championship Series, he batted .409 with two homers and 10 RBIs. He almost had a third home run off the Indians in Game 5 when he launched a deep fly ball that hit the top of the wall and bounced back onto the field. Ramirez, true to form, was already into his trot and wound up with a 375-foot single.

Whatever else Manny Ramirez is, he is a lock for Cooperstown. His remarkable consistency put him in the top ten in MVP voting for eight consecutive seasons (1998–05), something not even Barry Bonds or Alex Rodriguez has ever accomplished.

alex RIOS

Back when he was playing Double-A ball in New Haven, Connecticut, Alex Rios took a bat and smashed a hole clean through his locker. Years later, he still remembers the incident; he just can't recall what prompted the outburst. That's the kind of intensity Rios was known for. It didn't matter whether he watched strike three or lined out sharply to left field — an out was an out, and it was unacceptable. Coaches and scouts in the Blue Jays system knew that their young prospect had unlimited potential, but they worried that his intolerance of failure might paralyze him. Baseball, after all, is a game where great hitters fail seven times out of ten.

Rios was born in Alabama, though his parents returned to their native Puerto Rico when he was still a baby. Like many teenagers, Rios enjoyed hanging out with his friends and didn't always devote his full energy to baseball. His father, however, drove home the message that a pro career would give him opportunities he would never have on the island. When Toronto selected him in the first round of the 1999 draft, he devoted himself to improving his skills. The scouting reports hailed his smooth right-handed swing, his strong throwing arm and his speed, but he showed no signs of becoming a power hitter: during his first four years in the minors he hit six homers in 1,450 at-bats. In 2003, however — the year he totaled his locker in New Haven — he had an MVP season (.352, 11 homers, 83 RBIs) and was called up to the Blue Jays

$ 24.95
GATE SECTION **2**
UPPER
NN18 SEAT
T1FF267
25JUNE08

CAREER HIGHLIGHTS

- posted a combined .505 slugging percentage in 2006 and 2007

- logged 11 outfield assists in 2007 and was deemed to have the best right-field arm by *The Hardball Times*

- selected to the AL All-Star Team in 2006 and 2007

15 RIGHT FIELD

Alex RIOS

the following spring. While he batted a respectable .286 in his rookie season, he hit all of one home run in 460 plate appearances. He also sent a message to opposing baserunners by gunning down 11 from right field in only 108 games.

As Toronto's everyday right fielder in 2005, Rios upped his home run total to 10, but hit .262 and showed impatience at the plate by drawing a mere 28 walks. He finally showcased his talents the following year, batting .330 with 15 homers in the first half alone. He was selected to the AL All-Star Team, but was forced to sit out with an unusual injury: he fouled a ball off his leg on June 29 and sat out the next match when the pain got worse. It turned out that Rios had a staph infection that ended up sidelining him for a month. He wasn't the same after his return. In his second game back in late July, he struck out five times, and over the final months he hit only two more homers and watched his average drop 28 points.

The 26-year-old Rios rebounded in 2007 with another solid first half and was named to his second All-Star Team as the Blue Jays' only representative. The selection seemed to energize Rios: in Toronto's last game before the break, he came to the plate in the bottom of the ninth against the first-place Cleveland Indians. With score tied 0–0 and a runner on second, he promptly

lined a single into center field for his first walk-off hit. The next day, Rios was in San Francisco for the Home Run Derby, alongside the best power hitters in the game. Incredibly, the player who hit a single home run three seasons before stepped up and pounded five in the first round (tied for first), and then stunned everyone in the second round by launching a dozen taters, more than any other competitor's single-round total. Rios eventually lost to Vladimir Guerrero in the final, but he left an impression. "What he did in that Home Run Derby, everybody across the country was watching," said Arizona Diamondbacks second baseman Orlando Hudson, a former teammate. "That opened the door."

Like Guerrero (who failed to hit a single home run that July), Rios was haunted by the curse of the Home Run Derby in the second half, and he hit just seven long balls in the final three months. But his overall production was better than ever: he batted over .340 in both July and August, with 24 multi-hit games during those two months. Rios finished the 2007 season with 43 doubles, 24 home runs, 320 total bases, 85 RBIs, 17 steals and a .354 OBP, all career highs. No longer known for outbursts of locker-smashing anger, and never paralyzed by impossible expectations, Alex Rios has matured into a focused competitor with a bright future in the Toronto outfield.

grady SIZEMORE

CLEVELAND INDIANS ◆ AL Central

Baseball scouts know there is no shortage of teenage players with tremendous talent, but it takes more than physical skill to succeed at the major-league level. The best prospects don't just put up big numbers, they also demonstrate patience, maturity and competitive drive. The Montreal Expos scouts who watched Grady Sizemore play at Cascade High School near Seattle knew they had found a kid with the whole package. Not only did Sizemore bat .457 in his senior year — not to mention graduating as the football team's all-time leading rusher — he also had a 3.5 grade point average. However, Sizemore's most attractive quality was his winning attitude: he dove for balls in the outfield whether it was a tie game or a rout, and he hustled on every batted ball whether it was in the gap or grounded to second base.

The Expos drafted Sizemore in 2000 and he immediately showed his good strike-zone judgment, collecting 81 walks in 123 games in Class-A. He hit just six home runs in his first three minor-league seasons, but the consensus was that the power would come. It just wouldn't come in Montreal. In 2002 the Expos dealt him and three other players to the Cleveland Indians for Bartolo Colon and Tim Drew. Colon lasted half a season with Montreal, while Drew's career spanned all of 35 games. Sizemore, meanwhile, has become a franchise player in Cleveland.

The 22-year-old outfielder made his first appearance with the big club in July 2004. Three days after being called up, Sizemore came into a game against Kansas City as a pinch runner and later found himself at the plate in the bottom of the ninth with the score tied 3–3. He won the game with an RBI single. In 42 games that season he batted just .246, but the Indians were impressed enough to give him the center field job in 2005, replacing Juan Gonzalez, who had suffered a career-ending injury. Sizemore met the challenge by batting .289 with 22 home runs, 22 steals and 111 runs scored.

The following year, Sizemore established himself as an MVP in the making. Now a fixture atop the Indians' lineup, he played all 162 games and led the league in doubles (53), extra-base hits (92), runs scored (132) and total chances in the outfield (419), all while belting 28 home runs. As for his trademark hustle, Sizemore grounded into a double play only twice in 751 plate appearances and dived for balls on the warning track even when the Indians were out of the playoff picture.

Most of Sizemore's numbers dipped slightly in 2007, though he swiped a career-high 33 bases, and his outfield acrobatics won him his first Gold Glove. Most importantly, he led the Indians to the best record in the majors and a valiant postseason run that ended with a Game 7 loss to the Red Sox in the ALCS.

A quick glance at Sizemore's numbers — a career average of .283, and enough power to slug .500 or better — may suggest that he's more suited to the number-three spot in the batting order. But if the value of a leadoff hitter lies in his ability to get on base and score runs, Sizemore stacks up against anyone in the majors. His willingness to walk (he drew 101 free passes in 2007) makes his OBP comparable to Seattle's Ichiro Suzuki, whose career batting average is 50 points higher.

Sizemore also averages more runs per game than his Mariners counterpart, not least because his extra-base power gets him into scoring position more often than a singles hitter like Ichiro. To become a first-rate leadoff man, however, Sizemore will need to make contact more often — he has been among the AL's top four in strikeouts in each of his three full seasons.

His list of accomplishments makes it easy to forget that Sizemore didn't turn 25 until late in the 2007 season. Looking ahead to his prime years in Cleveland, what this budding superstar really wants is to win a championship for the Indians, who came close in 1995, 1997 and 2007 but haven't won a World Series since 1948. His $23-million contract is good until at least 2011, so Sizemore will have several seasons to try and lead them there.

$ 24.95
GATE 87
SECTION FIELD
SEAT AA23
A23SH54
15JUNE08

CAREER HIGHLIGHTS

- youngest player to collect 90 extra-base hits and 20 steals in one season (2006, age 24)
- first player since 1937 to collect 50 doubles, 10 triples and 25 home runs in the same season (2006)
- selected to the AL All-Star Team in 2006 and 2007

24 CENTER FIELD

Grady SIZEMORE

alfonso SORIANO

CHICAGO CUBS ◆ NL Central

In the spring of 2006 Alfonso Soriano was one of the most unpopular players in baseball. The previous December, the Texas Rangers had traded Soriano to the Washington Nationals, and he immediately took his new team to salary arbitration. He lost, but was still awarded $10 million for the upcoming season, the largest amount ever awarded by an arbitrator. Baseball fans are accustomed to the eye-popping salaries of the game's superstars, but most get surly when those players behave like spoiled children. Soriano did just that on March 20, 2006, when manager Frank Robinson asked the second baseman to start a spring training game in left field. When the $10-million man refused, *Sports Illustrated* called him "a selfish, greedy prima donna." The Nationals did one better: they threatened to place him on the disqualified list, which would cause Soriano to forfeit his salary and make him ineligible for free agency at the end of the season. Two days later, he relented and went out to left field.

To his credit, Soriano put the incident behind him immediately, and he later admitted that his reluctance came from a fear that he would embarrass himself in the unfamiliar position. When the season began, he played well enough to lead the loop in outfield assists come early July (he threw out 22 runners that season) and he earned a starting spot on the NL All-Star Team. Almost everyone believed Soriano would be traded before the deadline, but by that time he had won over fans and teammates with his positive attitude. Soriano stayed in Washington and had an outstanding year, leading the league with 89 extra-base hits and smacking a career-best 46 home runs. He also stole 41 bases, becoming the fourth player to collect 40 homers and 40 steals in the same season, and he finished sixth in the MVP voting — a remarkable result considering that Washington's RFK Stadium is notoriously hostile to hitters, and that the Nationals finished dead last in the NL East.

It was only natural for Alfonso Soriano to think of

CAREER HIGHLIGHTS

- only player to collect 40 homers, 40 doubles and 40 steals in one season (2006)

- set major-league record with 13 leadoff home runs in 2003

- only player to hit All-Star Game home runs for three different teams (Yankees, Rangers, Cubs)

12 LEFT FIELD

Alfonso SORIANO

himself as a middle infielder. He was born in San Pedro de Macoris, a town in the Dominican Republic that is nicknamed "the shortstop factory." At just 19 years old, he began his career in Japan — at shortstop, naturally — before being acquired by the Yankees. New York wasn't about to displace Derek Jeter, however, so they groomed Soriano as a second baseman. He made his MLB debut late in 1999 and recorded his first hit on September 24: a walk-off home run in the 11th inning of a game against Tampa Bay.

Soriano played his first full season in the big leagues in 2001. Everyone knew he could run, and his 43 steals were a Yankee record for rookies. He also showed more pop in his bat than your average second baseman, as he slugged 18 homers and drove in 73 runs. In the postseason, he belted a ninth-inning homer to beat the Mariners in Game 4 of the ALCS, and added another walk-off hit in the 12th inning of Game 5 in the World Series. But Soriano was just warming up. The next year he moved to the leadoff spot and batted .300 with

39 home runs, 102 RBIs and a league-leading 209 hits, then followed that up with 38 homers and 91 RBIs in 2003. With more than 35 steals in each season, Soriano was a rare combination of power and speed.

Before the 2004 season, Soriano was dealt to the Rangers in a blockbuster trade that brought Alex Rodriguez to the Yankees. In his second year in Texas, Soriano went deep 36 times to join Ryne Sandberg as the only two second basemen to have four straight seasons with at least 25 home runs.

After his monster season with the Nationals, a number of clubs expressed interest in the free agent, but few expected him to end up where he did: Soriano signed an eight-year, $136-million deal with the Chicago Cubs. The Cubs new manager, Lou Piniella, originally moved him to center field, though he ended up spending most of 2007 in left. Hampered by an early season hamstring injury, his production was less than expected in April and May, and after being named NL Player of the Month in June (.336, 11 homers, 18 RBIs), he tore his quadricep in August and wound up on the DL. But he finished with a red-hot September, pounding 14 home runs (a team record for one month), including seven leadoff dingers, setting a new MLB mark for a single month. The late surge helped Chicago win the NL Central, but like the rest of the Cubs, he couldn't get it going in the NLDS and his club bowed out to the Diamondbacks in the three straight.

ichiro SUZUKI

Ichiro Suzuki's career has included a string of impressive accomplishments, but the most remarkable is this: he is the only player in baseball history who can claim to be the greatest leadoff hitter of two different decades, on two different continents.

Ichiro, like Madonna, Elvis and other great artists, is instantly recognized by his first name, which he wears on the back of his jersey in place of his surname. In 1994 he became a regular with the Orix Blue Wave of the Pacific League, one of Japan's two premier loops. He often gave his coaches fits with his unorthodox swing, during which he kicked his front leg up and back as the pitch approached, a style he has since modified. Back then it worked, though: during his first full season he collected 210 hits and a .385 average, both league records. He went on to win the batting title seven times in the Pacific League, as well as picking up seven Gold Gloves for his stellar play in the outfield.

In 2000 the Seattle Mariners paid the Blue Wave $13 million for the right to negotiate with Ichiro, and on November 18 he signed with the Mariners and became the first Japanese hitting star to play every day in North America. There was no shortage of predictions that Ichiro would fall flat. Being five-foot-nine and slightly built may have been fine in Japan, but could he cut it in the hard-hitting American League?

It didn't take long for him to silence

the doubters. Ichiro picked up four hits in the Mariners' opening series in 2001, and the following week he threw a 200-foot bullet from right field to gun down a runner at third base. Some sportswriters said it was the finest throw they had ever seen. Ichiro's rookie season, in fact, was one of the greatest debuts ever. He won the batting crown with a .350 average, led the league with 56 stolen bases, and picked up 242 hits — no one had collected that many since 1930. Ichiro became just the second rookie ever to be named MVP. He also added a Gold Glove and led the majors with more than three million All-Star votes, many from Japanese fans who sent their support via the Internet. Along the way, the Mariners won 116 games to tie the major-league record for most victories.

Ichiro's average dropped off during the next two seasons, but only by his impossible standards — he still hit .321 and .312 with more than 200 hits in both years, becoming the third major leaguer to reach that mark in each of his first three seasons. Then, in 2004, he had a record-smashing year at the plate as he lined, chopped, bunted, blooped and hustled out 262 hits, surpassing George Sisler's mark of 257, which had stood for 83 years. He won his second batting title with a .372 average, tops in the majors.

Ichiro remains a serious threat to steal, even as he approaches his mid-30s. Not only is he among the league leaders in thefts, but he's also one of the least likely to get caught. In 2006, he swiped 45 bags while getting thrown out just twice, including a stretch of 39 in a row. The following year, the 33-year-old stole 37 in 45 attempts.

Ichiro does have his detractors. He truly is a singles hitter — during his 262-hit season, he had just 24 doubles, 5 triples and 8 homers — and he drives in few runs, even for a leadoff man. During one stretch in 2006, he went 86 at-bats without an RBI. While he rarely strikes out, he walks even less, and his on-base percentage (.379) is lower than one would expect from someone with a career batting average of .333.

Brushing aside that criticism, most Mariners fans rejoiced in 2007 when Ichiro — now in center field — signed a five-year contract extension, just days after he became the first player to hit an inside-the-park home run in an All-Star Game. His .351 average, the second-highest of his career, was good for second in the league, and on September 3 he sent a Roger Clemens pitch over the wall for his 200th hit of the season, making it seven straight seasons with 200 or more, tying Wade Boggs' modern record. After collecting 1,278 hits during nine seasons in Japan, Ichiro is well on his way to joining MLB's 3,000-hit club, which would make him the most prolific hit man in baseball history.

$ 24.95
GATE 54
SECTION UPPER
SEAT KK16
L2VP843
28MAY08

CAREER HIGHLIGHTS

- won seven Gold Gloves in Japan and seven more in North America

- tied major-league record with seven straight 200-hit seasons (2001–07)

- leads all active major leaguers in career batting average (.333)

51 CENTER FIELD

Ichiro SUZUKI

nick
SWISHER

Nick Swisher is what sportscasters like to call a character guy. Other players can pound 35 home runs a season — as Swisher did in 2006 — but few of them seem to be having as much fun while doing it.

Swisher is a second-generation big-leaguer: his father, Steve, was a catcher and first-round draft pick in 1973. When Nick was born in Columbus, Ohio, on November 25, 1980, his father had just completed his second season with the St. Louis Cardinals. The younger Swisher went to Ohio State University, and in 2000 he was selected Freshman of the Year in the Big Ten conference, batting .299 with 10 home runs. In his next two years at Ohio State, he batted .322 and .348 and attracted scouts with his versatility. Not only was he adept in the outfield and at first base, but he was a left-handed thrower who could switch hit — a rare breed. Everyone who watched Nick Swisher also noticed his approachability and his ready smile. This was a kid who loved to play baseball. No one thought more highly of Swisher than Oakland's unorthodox general manager, Billy Beane, who chose him in the first round, 16th overall. (Beane's pursuit of Swisher was featured at length in Michael Lewis' popular book *Moneyball*.)

Being a first-round pick placed a lot of pressure on Swisher, but he embraced the challenge. He knew the A's were obsessive about grooming their young hitters to learn the strike zone and be selective, and he pleased them by drawing 78 walks

CAREER HIGHLIGHTS

- led AL rookies in homers, RBIs, walks and extra-base hits in 2005

- set Oakland record for most home runs by a switch hitter (35) in 2006 and is the team's all-time leader in that category

- one of six AL players to draw 100 bases on balls in 2007

33 RIGHT/CENTER FIELD

Nick SWISHER

in 127 minor-league games in 2003, compiling a .363 on-base percentage to go with his 15 home runs. Promoted to Triple-A the following season, he hit 29 homers, drove in 92 runs and added 103 walks for an OBP of .406. Swisher was rewarded with a September call-up, and in his big-league debut in Toronto he smacked a double in the fourth inning en route to a 7–4 win over the Blue Jays. Before the month was out, he had played all three outfield positions as well as first base and DH, and had a realistic shot at cracking the A's everyday lineup the following year.

At training camp in the spring of 2005, Swisher worked harder than he ever had before, earning himself a spot in right field on Opening Day. Though he batted just .236 in his rookie season, Swisher drove in 74 runs and hit 21 long balls — which, he liked to point out to his dad, was one more than the elder Swisher had hit in his entire career.

In his sophomore year in 2006, Swisher burst out of the gates with 10 homers in April. He finished the season with 35 four-baggers to go along with 95 RBIs, despite hitting .190 with runners in scoring position and striking out 152 times. Overall he batted a mediocre .254, but his 97 bases on balls gave him an impressive OBP of .372. He became the first Oakland player ever to start more than 70 games at two different positions, and wound up appearing in 80 games in the outfield and 90 at first base. More important for a team-oriented player like Swisher, the A's finished first in the AL West and swept the Minnesota Twins in the Division Series before being ousted by Detroit in the ALCS.

Before the 2007 campaign began, Swisher adopted an unconventional workout regimen: instead of spending his time in the gym, he retreated to his Ohio farm, where he chopped wood and swung a sledgehammer to bulk up. As things turned out, his home run and RBI numbers were down in 2007, but so were his strikeouts. Meanwhile, he improved to 36 doubles, 100 bases on balls and a career-high OBP of .381, which offset his .262 batting average. That was enough to win over the Chicago White Sox, who swung a deal for Swisher in the offseason and installed him as their new center fielder.

Infield
FLYERS

garrett ATKINS

COLORADO ROCKIES ◆ NL West

CAREER HIGHLIGHTS

- led the Rockies in RBIs in 2005 and 2006
- one of only two NL players to finish in the top 10 in batting average, RBI, runs, OBP and slugging in 2006
- posted back-to-back seasons with a .300-plus average and at least 25 home runs and 110 RBIs

27 THIRD BASE

Garrett ATKINS

Some players seem to fly under the radar year after year. In 2006 and 2007 Rockies third baseman Garrett Atkins hit a combined .315 with 54 home runs, 83 doubles and 231 RBIs, while David Wright, his counterpart on the New York Mets, batted .318, slugged 56 long balls and 82 two-baggers while driving in 223 runs. Despite these almost identical numbers, however, Wright has been named to the All-Star Team twice, won the 2007 Silver Slugger and finished in the top nine in MVP voting in both seasons. Atkins, meanwhile, has never won a league award and garners a fraction of Wright's media attention. Even in Colorado, the soft-spoken and laid-back corner infielder labors in the shadow of Matt Holliday.

It wasn't always this way for Atkins, who was one of the highest-profile ballplayers in the country during his college years. Drafted by the Mets in 1997, he did not sign and instead enrolled at UCLA for three years.

As a sociology major, he could have done his thesis on the public humiliation of pitchers: he batted .369 during his tenure and was the only three-time All-American in UCLA's history. When draft time came around again in 2000, the right-handed slugger with the textbook swing was selected by the Rockies in the fifth round.

After three years in the minors, Atkins was invited to spring training in 2003 and proceeded to bat .525 in 23 Cactus League games, setting a franchise record. The big club wasn't ready to give him a job quite yet, however, and he played most of the year in Triple-A.

When the Rockies called him up in August, Atkins struggled badly, hitting .159 in 25 games. He was back to Triple-A for 2004 and adopted a more open stance that helped him turn on inside pitches. The results were dramatic: he led all of minor-league baseball with a .366 average and smacked a league-best 43 doubles. Called up again in September, he started games at third base, first base and left field and went 10-for-28 (.357) at the plate.

Despite his big season, Atkins found himself in a tough spot heading into 2005. While he could play first base, he wasn't about to displace Todd Helton in the Rockies' lineup. And third base was occupied by Vinnie Castilla, a charter member of the expansion franchise and the National League's reigning RBI leader. To make things worse, one of Colorado's other top prospects, the 19-year-old Ian Stewart, was also a third baseman and had hit 30 home runs in Class-A in 2004.

Fortunately for Atkins, Castilla signed with Washington during the offseason, opening a spot on the roster in 2005. The rookie third baseman started the season on the disabled list with a strained hamstring, but showed no sign of ill health that June when he batted .364, slugged .533 and drove in 26 runs on the way to being named Rookie of the Month. When the year was out, Atkins had collected 89 RBIs to become the only freshman in franchise history to lead the team in that category.

Atkins had a breakout year in 2006, bookending the season by winning Player of the Week honors

in both the first and last weeks of the campaign. In between he wasn't so bad either. He kept his average above .300 all season, but kicked it into overdrive in the second half, rapping out a major-league-best 102 hits to finish at .329, fourth in the league. He more than doubled his home run total from the previous year, going yard 29 times, and batted .341 with runners in scoring position, all of which added up to 120 runs driven in. While his teammate and good friend Matt Holliday got most of the media attention — as well as a 2007 contract that paid him 11 times more than Atkins — it was the third baseman who had the edge in batting average, doubles, OPS and RBIs on the year.

Both Atkins and the Rockies, not coincidentally, started slowly but finished with a bang in the 2007 regular season. On June 1, the club was in last place, 7½ games back in the NL West, while Atkins was batting .223 with three home runs. But he was transformed in the second half: he rolled out a .349 clip after the All-Star break, including a torrid .398 in the final month as the Rockies won 14 of their final 15 to pull off one of the most improbable postseason berths in recent memory. Atkins' hot bat cooled off dramatically in the postseason, however. Making his October debut, he batted .175 during the club's quest for its first championship. His only homer of the playoffs, an eighth-inning two-run shot in Game 4 of the World Series, narrowed Boston's lead to one, but it was too little, too late, as the Red Sox went on to sweep the Rockies.

lance BERKMAN

When Lance Berkman moved from the outfield to first base in 2005, he replaced franchise player Jeff Bagwell, who called it quits after that season. Playing to Berkman's right in the Houston infield was second baseman Craig Biggio, who retired in 2007 after 20 seasons with the Astros. The departure of the original Killer B's has left Berkman as the new face of the team, a role that suits him perfectly. Not only is he an affable, well-liked teammate who has already established several club records, but he also has one quality that neither of his predecessors shared: Berkman was born and bred in the Lone Star State. "I love Texas and it loves me back," he likes to say.

The Astros' slugger was born in Waco and grew up in Austin and New Braunfels, a small city outside San Antonio. As a child, he displayed a rare combination: he threw left-handed, but batted right. Coached by his dad, he learned to switch-hit by taking countless practice swings at a tire he hung from a tree in his backyard. By the time he attended Rice University in Houston, he had a finely honed stroke from both sides of the plate — indeed, he has since become far more dangerous as a left-handed hitter.

Primarily a first baseman in college and the minors, Berkman broke in with the Astros as a corner outfielder, since no one was going to supplant Bagwell just yet. He started the 2000 season in Triple-A, but was called up in May and hit 21 home runs

$ 24.95
GATE 4
SECTION FIELD
SEAT BB2
25JUNE08
B00GR12

CAREER HIGHLIGHTS

- only switch hitter other than Mickey Mantle to post two seasons with 40 or more home runs
- holds NL single-season records for RBIs (136 in 2006) and extra-base hits (94 in 2001) by a switch hitter
- is the Astros all-time leader in slugging (.559) and batting average (.300)

17 FIRST BASE

Lance BERKMAN

in 353 at-bats. The following year, playing mostly in left field, Berkman had a magnificent season, with a .331 average, 34 homers, 126 RBIs and a 1.050 OPS, still a career high. He led the NL with 55 doubles, becoming the first switch hitter to record 50 doubles and 30 homers in a season. The Astros went 93–69 to win the NL Central that year, but were swept by the Atlanta Braves in the Division Series.

Switching to center field for much of 2002 — an unusual position for a player whose bulky frame inspired the nickname "Fat Elvis" — Berkman struck for 42 home runs and 128 RBIs, earning his second straight All-Star appearance. His numbers fell off the next year, but he rebounded in 2004 to post a career-best OBP of .450, thanks to 127 walks and 172 hits. The Astros had a huge second half that year and grabbed the wild card spot, this time ousting the Braves before bowing out in a thrilling seven-game NLCS against the St. Louis Cardinals. Berkman picked up four homers and 12 RBIs in the postseason, but it wasn't enough.

In the 2004 offseason, Berkman suffered a lapse in judgment: he played a game of flag football with his church group and tore a ligament in his knee. He missed 27 games at the start of 2005 (during which

Houston went 11–16) and then returned to lead the Astros to another wild card and their third playoff meeting with the Braves. The Astros won two of the first three games, but trailed 6–1 in the eighth inning of Game 4 when Berkman came to the plate with the bases loaded. Batting left-handed, he smacked an opposite-field grand slam to narrow the margin. The Astros tied it in the ninth and then won the series when Chris Burke, who had pinch-run for Berkman, hit a walk-off homer in the 18th inning. They went on to defeat the Cardinals to earn their first-ever World Series appearance. Despite Berkman's six RBIs in the first three games, however, the Chicago White Sox took four straight from the Astros.

While his team missed the postseason in 2006, Berkman had perhaps his best campaign to date, batting .315 and establishing career highs in homers (45), slugging (.621) and RBIs (136, a club record). Then everything went sour in 2007, as Houston slipped to an awful 73–89 record in baseball's weakest division. Berkman was bothered by a sore left hand all year — the result of being repeatedly jammed with inside pitches — but still finished with 34 homers and 102 RBIs. If the Astros are to return to contention, they will need Berkman's bat to take them there.

miguel CABRERA

Miguel Cabrera experienced a baptism by fastball during the 2003 World Series. Just 20 years old, the Florida Marlins' rookie walked to the plate in the first inning of Game 4 to face future Hall of Famer Roger Clemens. Cabrera swung through two pitches to get behind 1–2, and then the Rocket brushed him back with a high heater, knocking the youngster on his backside. One might have forgiven Cabrera if he felt intimidated, but he never lost his composure. Instead, he got up, fouled off two pitches and then hit the next one into the right-field seats for a two-run homer. The Marlins went on to win the game, and then took the next two to complete their second World Series championship.

Cabrera first caught the eye of Florida scouts while he was a teenager in Maracay, Venezuela. Although he was a shortstop at the time, the organization soon began grooming him as a third baseman. By mid-2003 he was batting .365 in Triple-A and the Marlins decided to see what he could do at the big-league level — the hope was that he would provide a boost to a team that was loaded with underachieving talent. On June 18 Florida was 34–39 and in last place in the NL East. Cabrera made his debut two days later, and after going 0-for-4 in the first nine innings, he belted a game-winning homer in the 11th for his first major-league hit. Playing the outfield and later covering third base when Mike Lowell was injured, he got some big hits down the stretch, posting a .375 average with runners in scoring position. With Cabrera in the lineup the Marlins took over the wild card lead on September 8 and went on to build a 56–31 record the rest of the way, riding the momentum all the way to the Fall Classic.

The Marlins' 2004 season was a disappointment, save for Cabrera's emergence as the best young hitter in the league. Still only 21, he batted .294 and led the club with 33 homers, 112 RBIs, 101 runs, 68 walks and a .512 slugging percentage. Cabrera played in the

outfield all year, as well as through most of 2005, when he logged even better offensive numbers. He upped his average to .323 and again stroked 33 home runs, while adding 43 doubles and 116 runs to win his first Silver Slugger Award.

Cabrera challenged the Pirates' Freddie Sanchez for the 2006 batting title right to the final week of the season, eventually finishing second at .339. He also swatted 26 homers and slugged .568 while setting a club record with 50 doubles — good for his second Silver Slugger, this time as a third baseman. Cabrera has always been concerned about his propensity to strike out, and in 2006 he improved in that department for the second straight year. He also drew a career-high 86 bases on balls, leading to a .430 OBP, third-best in the league. He had become such a threat that he was walked intentionally 27 times, and that number should have been 28 but for one of the oddest plays of the season. In the 10th inning of a game against Baltimore in June, the Marlins had Hanley Ramirez on second with first base open, and the Orioles decided to put Cabrera on. But as pitcher Todd Williams lobbed the first ball toward the catcher's outstretched mitt, Cabrera reached out and punched it into center field, sending Ramirez home with the winning run.

In his second full year at third base, Cabrera put up MVP-type numbers for the fourth straight season: a .320 average and career highs in home runs (34) and RBIs (119). The only worrisome aspect of his game was his declining skill on defense (highlighted by a league-high 23 errors at third base in 2007), which may have something to do with his ballooning weight: he was 185 pounds when he broke into the big leagues and is now listed at 240. But none of that seemed to faze the Detroit Tigers, who acquired Cabrera and pitcher Dontrelle Willis during the Winter Mettings that year in exchange for a package of prospects.

prince FIELDER

As home run hitters go, Prince Fielder has good genes. His dad is Cecil Fielder, the two-time American League home run champion who pounded 51 for the Detroit Tigers in 1990, and then 44 more the following year. Prince often went on the road with his father and sometimes took batting practice. When he was 12 years old, he even hit a ball over the right-field fence in the old Tiger Stadium.

The younger Fielder inherited not only his father's home run power, but also his body type. Cecil's weight eventually derailed his career, and by high school Prince was already over 300 pounds. He worked out hard and dropped a lot of extra baggage, but his weight was such a concern among scouts that some teams wouldn't touch him when he became eligible for the draft in 2002. The Milwaukee Brewers, however, surprised everyone by taking him seventh overall, even passing over Scott Kazmir and Nick Swisher. Eighty home runs later, that choice is looking awfully good.

Fielder lit up pitchers at every minor league level from the time he was 18. After batting .390 with 10 home runs in 41 games in Rookie ball, he quickly moved through the ranks, and his 28 homers in Triple-A earned him some at-bats with the Brewers in 2005. On June 25, in the sixth inning of a game against the Minnesota Twins, Fielder was called on to pinch-hit with two runners on and the Brewers trailing 5–4. The 21-year-old met the challenge by driving a pitch over

the wall in left-center for his first major-league home run, which held up as the game winner. Fielder collected his second long ball on August 31, and this one was even more dramatic. Once again coming off the bench with his team trailing by a run — this time in the bottom of the ninth against Pittsburgh — he parked one in the right field seats for a two-run walk-off homer.

The Brewers saw enough in their young prospect that they traded away Lyle Overbay to make room at first base in 2006. Fielder went to work immediately, batting .344 in April with 10 multi-hit games, five home runs and 16 RBIs to take NL Rookie of the Month honors. During one wild game against Cincinnati that month, Fielder came to the plate in the sixth inning after four of his teammates had already gone deep, and promptly pounded a home run of his own. It was the fifth time in MLB history that a team has hit five in one frame. Not wanting to be typecast as an all-or-nothing power hitter, Fielder kept his average at .300 or better until June 12 before cooling off in the second half and finishing at .271, with a healthy .347 OBP. He led all NL rookies with 28 home runs and was a bright spot on a team that finished fourth in their division.

Hardly anyone gave

Milwaukee a chance before the 2007 season. But the Brew Crew grabbed hold of first place in the NL Central on April 21 and built their lead as Fielder batted .321 with 13 home runs in May. By the break, the slugger had surpassed his home-run total of the previous year and managed to edge out Albert Pujols and Derek Lee as the starting first baseman on the National League All-Star Team. Milwaukee kept on winning in the second half, largely on the strength of their power hitting (the team led the NL in home runs). On August 17, the Chicago Cubs finally caught them, but the Brewers would not roll over. Fielder did everything he could to keep his team in the hunt, pounding 20 homers in the final two months, but the Cubs took over first place for good in mid-September.

Prince Fielder has an uneasy relationship with his father these days, and has openly admitted that he would like to eclipse what Cecil accomplished. By the end of his remarkable sophomore year, the younger Fielder had pounded an even 50, one short of his dad's career high, but a remarkable figure that topped the National League — making this prince a home-run king.

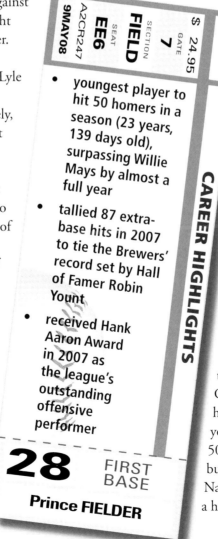

$ 24.95
GATE 7
SECTION FIELD
SEAT EE6
A2CR247
9MAY08

CAREER HIGHLIGHTS

- **youngest player to hit 50 homers in a season (23 years, 139 days old), surpassing Willie Mays by almost a full year**

- **tallied 87 extra-base hits in 2007 to tie the Brewers' record set by Hall of Famer Robin Yount**

- **received Hank Aaron Award in 2007 as the league's outstanding offensive performer**

28
FIRST BASE
Prince FIELDER

nomar GARCIAPARRA

Here's a trivia question with a surprising answer: which American League shortstop had the highest combined OPS from 1997 to 2000? Was it Derek Jeter, the league's top rookie in 1996, who quickly established himself as one of the best all-around players in the game? Or maybe Alex Rodriguez, who collected 148 home runs during that span? Wrong on both counts. The answer is Nomar Garciaparra, who posted a .963 OPS over his first four incredible seasons.

Garciaparra was born in Whittier, California, and was given his unusual moniker when his Mexican-born father, Ramon, reversed the letters of his own name. Always tall and thin, he was hardly built for power when he entered the Red Sox farm system at barely 160 pounds. But Nomar had bulked up somewhat by the time he played his first full season in the majors in 1997, and he made one of the greatest debuts ever for a middle infielder. Batting atop the lineup, he hit .306 with 30 homers (a major-league record for rookie shortstops), drove in 98 runs (an MLB record for leadoff hitters, broken in 2002 by Alfonso Soriano) and had a 30-game hit streak, the longest ever for an AL first-year player. He was a no-brainer for Rookie of the Year.

Proving he was no fluke, Garciaparra improved in 1998 to .323 with 35 homers and 122 RBIs. He would never match the home run totals of his first two seasons, but Nomar was just getting warmed up as a productive hitter who could absolutely dominate a game. On May 10, 1999, he

CAREER HIGHLIGHTS

- one of five players (and the only shortstop) to hit 30 or more home runs in each of his first two seasons

- elected to five AL All-Star Teams (1997, 1999, 2000, 2002–03) and one NL All-Star Team (2006)

- ranks sixth among active players in career batting average (.315)

FIRST BASE

5

Nomar GARCIAPARRA

became the 11th player in history to hit two grand slams in the same match, and he sandwiched them around a two-run shot for a 10-RBI night. On July 23, 2002 — his 29th birthday — Garciaparra hit two home runs in the third inning of a game against Tampa Bay, then came up in the fourth and added a grand slam.

Nomar won his first batting crown in 1999, when he hit .357. The year ended on a painful note, however, when he was hit on the wrist by a pitch in late September. The injury nagged him throughout the next season and beyond, and likely affected his home run power. Incredibly, Garciaparra still notched 51 doubles in 2000 and won his second straight batting title with a .372 average. The sore wrist required surgery in April 2001, causing him to miss almost the entire season in recovery. His average slipped to .310 in 2002, but he still managed 24 home runs and set a major-league record for shortstops with 56 doubles.

Nomar had good numbers again in 2003, but a contract dispute, coupled with the Red Sox' heartbreaking loss in the ALCS, created some bad blood with the fans who had once adored him. When he started 2004 on the DL after injuring his Achilles tendon in spring training, his relationship with the team fell apart, and the Sox shipped him to the Chicago Cubs. Boston went on to win the World Series without him.

The parade of injuries continued for Garciaparra, who played just 62 games with the Cubs before signing with the Los Angeles Dodgers in the offseason. Reunited with Grady Little, his former manager in Boston, Nomar played first base for the first time in his career and had a fine 2006, hitting .303 with 20 homers and 93 RBIs in just 121 contests. Always one to be at the center of dramatic games, he capped one of the most remarkable comebacks in recent memory on September 18 that year. Trailing San Diego 9–5 in the bottom of the ninth, the Dodgers hit four consecutive homers to tie it. Then, after the Padres went up 10–9 in the top of the 10th, Nomar hit a two-run shot in the bottom of the inning to win the game.

Garciaparra crashed back to earth in 2007. He was batting .280 with six home runs in mid-August when he went back on the DL with a calf strain. It now seems unlikely that he will join A-Rod and Jeter in Cooperstown, but at 34 years old, it's too soon to write off Nomar. His career may have one more triumphant return still to come.

ryan HOWARD

Ryan Howard found himself in a strange predicament at the end of 2004. After starting the year in Double-A, he was promoted to Triple-A and then played 19 games with the Phillies, hitting a combined 48 homers and driving in 136 runs. Despite those huge numbers, there was something blocking his way to becoming a major-league first baseman. That something was Jim Thome, who owned the job in Philadelphia and had hit 42 homers of his own in 2004, and 47 the year before.

Howard was used to being a big guy in the shadow of even bigger guys — at six-foot-four, he's the smallest of the three brothers in his family. At high school in St. Louis, he starred on the diamond, but went undrafted when scouts failed to notice his potential. Howard finally turned some heads in his junior year at Southwest Missouri State, when he hit 19 home runs in the short college season. The Phillies selected him in the fifth round in 2001, and two years later he tore up the Class-A Florida State League. When 2005 rolled around, Howard was hitting .371 with 16 home runs after 61 games in Triple-A, and was clearly ready for the big time.

Howard is too nice a guy to have wished for something bad to happen to Thome. But as fate would have it, the veteran slugger developed tendinitis in his elbow in July and was gone for the year. Howard was called up as his replacement and was determined to make the most of the opportunity. He had five hits,

including a home run, in his first three games and then gave his team postseason hopes with a tremendous run down the stretch, including 10 dingers in September, a record for first-year players. (The Phillies finished one game out in the wild card race.) Though he played just 88 games, Howard collected 22 homers, including two grand slams, and drove in 63 runs to win the NL Rookie of the Year Award.

The Phils were so smitten that they traded Thome in the offseason to make room for their young star, and Howard responded with a tremendous first half of 2006. He slammed 28 homers and tallied 71 RBIs before the break, earning a spot on the All-Star Team. For the fans who had not yet witnessed his power, that year's Home Run Derby was Howard's center stage: he smashed 23 taters, many of them prodigious, to win the contest.

Howard could have had a mediocre second half and he still would have finished with fine overall numbers. Instead, he got even better. He hit a torrid .355 after the All-Star Game and added 30 homers to finish with 58, tops in the majors. His 41 RBIs in August were the most a player had posted in one month since 1962, and his final total of 149 was the highest in either league. The Cardinals'

Albert Pujols also had a magnificent season, but it was Howard who got 20 of the 32 first-place votes to win the MVP award in his first full year.

Coming off a performance like that, it wasn't surprising that Howard appeared to be pressing when 2007 got under way. He missed 15 days in May with a strained quadriceps, and by June 1 he was batting .222 with a mere nine homers. But he bounced back to hit a combined .300 in June and July, with 10 home runs in each of those months, and continued to drive in runners with big hits as the Phillies bounced the New York Mets to win the NL East on the final day of the season. His biggest personal milestone came on June 27, when he turned around a pitch from the Reds' Aaron Harang and hit a moon shot to straightaway center for the 100th home run of his career. By September, he was leading the loop in RBIs and finished with 136, one behind leader Matt Holliday.

Howard is an articulate, intelligent and outgoing young man who thinks deeply about how he can improve as a hitter. His left-handed swing is finely tuned, and as he develops he should be to able cut down on his strikeouts, now the biggest knock against his game. (He fanned 181 times in 2006, and set a major-league record with 199 in 2007.) About half of his long balls go over the center or left field fences, and his career .291 average demonstrates that he can adjust with the pitch and use the whole yard. So far, no one has built a ballpark that can contain Ryan Howard.

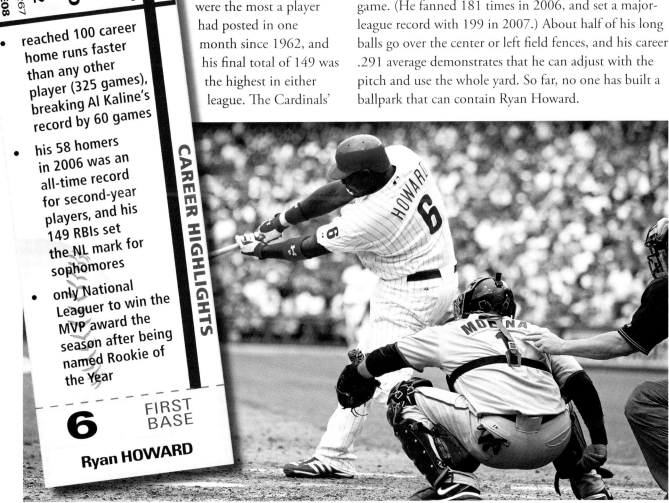

$ 24.95

GATE 27

SECTION FIELD

SEAT G32

U3CS267 2JUNE08

CAREER HIGHLIGHTS

- reached 100 career home runs faster than any other player (325 games), breaking Al Kaline's record by 60 games

- his 58 homers in 2006 was an all-time record for second-year players, and his 149 RBIs set the NL mark for sophomores

- only National Leaguer to win the MVP award the season after being named Rookie of the Year

6 FIRST BASE

Ryan HOWARD

derek JETER

NEW YORK YANKEES ◆ AL East

Derek Jeter isn't a native New Yorker, but he's a homegrown Yankee nonetheless. Jeter was born on the other side of the George Washington Bridge in Pequannock, New Jersey, and his childhood dream of wearing the pinstripes came true when he was selected sixth overall in the 1992 draft. He raced through the Yankees' farm system, and by 1996 he was their Opening Day shortstop. His arrival marked the beginning of a dynasty that would see the team win four World Series championships in five years.

In his debut season, Jeter compiled a .314 average to win Rookie of the Year honors, and then batted .361 in his first postseason. By 1998 he had evolved into one of the league's best-hitting middle infielders, as he smacked 204 hits, led the loop with 127 runs, and tallied 19 homers to break the club record for shortstops. He did even better the following season. After reaching base safely in the first 53 games of 1999, he scored 134 runs, had his first 100-RBI campaign and was the runner-up for the batting title with a .349 average. Jeter also earned two more rings as the Yankees steamrolled their way to back-to-back World Series wins in 1998 and 1999, thanks in part to his combined .353 clip in both Fall Classics.

The 26-year-old Jeter stroked a single in the final week of 2000 to become the second-youngest Yankee to reach 1,000 hits — only Mickey Mantle was younger. In his third All-Star appearance that year, he went 3-for-3 and was the game's MVP, but he saved his real magic for the postseason. He slugged .864 in the Subway Series against the Mets and was named World Series MVP as the Yankees completed the "three-peat." By that point, Jeter had learned not to make other plans for October: during his career he has played in 25 playoff series and has earned a reputation as a clutch player with his glove as well as his bat. In Game 3 of the 2001 Division Series against Oakland, he ran all the way across the diamond to retrieve an errant throw from right field, and then

flipped the ball to catcher Jorge Posada to nail Jeremy Giambi at home in one of the most creative plays in playoff history.

Jeter has never had an off-year at the plate — an injury in 2003 was the only thing that kept him from recording 12 straight seasons with at least 180 hits, 100 runs and 70 RBIs. He opened the 2004 season with the worst slump of his career — he didn't cross the Mendoza Line until May 26 — but rallied in the second half to finish at .294 with 23 homers and a personal-best 44 doubles. He put up similar numbers the next season before having arguably his best year in 2006, hitting .343, winning his first Silver Slugger and finishing second in the AL MVP voting. (He opened the postseason that year by going 5-for-5 with a homer and two doubles, but the Yankees lost the next three to the Detroit Tigers.) Jeter showed no signs of letting up in 2007, batting .322 and being voted to the All-Star Team for the eighth time.

Jeter is one of baseball's good guys, the embodiment of maturity and class. He is so well respected for his leadership qualities, in fact, that many fans and analysts outside of New York argue that he is overrated as a player, particularly when it comes to defense. While he has a strong arm and makes his share of brilliant plays — ESPN is still getting mileage out of his miraculous over-the-shoulder grab of a Trot Nixon blooper in 2004 — statistical gurus have rated his range among the worst in the majors. *Baseball Prospectus* ranked him dead last in 2001 and predicted that he would "join the ranks of the defensively horrific who win Gold Gloves because of their charisma, the occasional highlight reel play, exposure and their offensive production." Sure enough, Jeter — who has unquestionably improved his defense since then — won three straight Gold Gloves from 2004 to 2006.

Just don't try mentioning any of that criticism to Yankee fans. Derek Jeter is the heart of the most successful baseball team of the last dozen years, and what he means to his ball club can't be measured by statistics.

$ 24.95
GATE 2
SECTION 2
CLUB
SEAT D67
P5DS667
30CT08

CAREER HIGHLIGHTS

- only player to win All-Star Game MVP and World Series MVP in the same season (2000)

- holds major-league record for postseason hits (153) and runs (85), accomplished in 123 games

- only shortstop in MLB history to record six seasons of 200 or more hits

2 SHORTSTOP

Derek JETER

chipper JONES

ATLANTA BRAVES ◆ NL East

During spring training in 2005, Chipper Jones reflected on the previous year, the worst of his career. He had batted just .248 and spent most of the previous three seasons stuck in left field after establishing himself as a five-time All-Star at third base. "This is 12 years now that I've been playing, and I ain't playing 12 more," he told a reporter. "I'm on the backside of my career, I know that."

In the campaign that followed that comment, Jones went out and upped his average by almost 50 points. In 2006 he improved again to .324 and slugged .596, both well above his career averages. Then, at age 35, Jones finished second in the 2007 NL batting race with a .337 average, tallied a career-high 42 doubles and slugged .604. While pain has limited his playing time — Jones has spent five separate stints on the DL during his past three seasons — he has performed remarkably well when his body has allowed him into the lineup.

Chipper Jones is the quintessential franchise player, and the contract he signed in 2002 will almost certainly ensure that he will end his career in Atlanta, where the six-foot-four switch hitter debuted as a 21-year-old shortstop in 1993. (With the retirement of Craig Biggio in 2007, Jones is the active player with the longest tenure on a single club.) Jones looked to be a regular in the big-league lineup during the spring of 1994, but the budding star tore the anterior cruciate ligament in his left knee and missed the entire strike-shortened season. In his first full year with the Braves in 1995, Jones hit 23 home runs to finish as the runner-up for Rookie of the Year. He added three more long balls in the postseason as Atlanta won its one and only World Series during the team's incredible run of 14 consecutive division titles.

In 1996 Jones enjoyed the first of five seasons in which he batted over .300 with at least 30 homers and 100 RBIs, and he was starting to look like an MVP-caliber player. Sure enough, he put it all together in

1999: a .441 OBP, 45 homers (a league record for a switch hitter) and 110 RBIs, capturing the NL's top award in a landslide, with 29 of 32 first-place MVP votes. He won his first Silver Slugger that year, and then captured the hardware again in 2000 when he batted a sizzling .415 when swinging right-handed.

Chipper — his given name is Larry Wayne Jones Jr. — moved to the outfield for the 2002 and 2003 seasons to make room for the newly acquired Vinny Castilla. The Braves didn't sacrifice much on defense — Jones' range at the hot corner is below average — but the move was something of a failed experiment; Castilla didn't last long in Atlanta, and Jones was back at third in 2004. By now, nagging injuries were hampering his production after six straight seasons over .300 and eight in a row with more than 100 runs driven in. He played 109 games in 2005, and had the lowest home run and RBI output of his career.

Jones may be hobbling,

$ 24.95

GATE 17

SECTION UPPER

SEAT AA17

K9SS568

15JUNE08

CAREER HIGHLIGHTS

- only switch hitter in MLB history to combine a .300 lifetime batting average and 300 home runs

- first player to record a season with a .300 average and at least 40 doubles, 40 home runs, 100 walks, 100 runs, 100 RBIs and 20 steals (1999)

- one of three players to hit 20 or more home runs in each of their first 13 seasons

10

THIRD BASE

Chipper JONES

but he can still swing the bat, and he has achieved some impressive milestones in the past couple of seasons. In 2006 he collected his 1,144th RBI and his 1,901st hit to become the Atlanta Braves' all-time leader in both categories, and he smacked an extra-base hit in 14 straight games that year to tie a major-league record. He tallied his 2,000th hit in 2007, and put his name atop the club's all-time list in home runs with a big day on July 5. Facing the Dodgers in Los Angeles, Chipper came up batting right-handed in the sixth inning and hit his 371st dinger to tie Dale Murphy and put the Braves up 7–6 in the game. Two innngs later, he turned around and swatted number 372 from the left side.

Jones is on pace to become the only third baseman with a lifetime batting average over .300 to go along with 400 home runs. He is also racking up numbers that place him among the top switch hitters in National League history. Rather than being on the backside of his career, Chipper Jones is making the kind of late-career resurgence that often gives players the final nudge they need to make it to the Hall of Fame.

derrek LEE

25

CHICAGO CUBS ◆ NL Central

Derrek Lee was born in Sacramento, California, but his formative baseball experiences came in Japan. Both his uncle (a former major leaguer) and his father had long professional careers in the Japanese Pacific League, and Derrek would often spend his summers hanging out with them and watching how professionals played the game. By the time he was a teenager, Lee had developed into a top prospect, and in 1993 the San Diego Padres drafted him in the first round.

In 1996 Lee was mashing the ball in Double-A and was MVP of the Southern League with a .301 average and 34 homers. The Padres decided to call him up the following April, but he clearly wasn't ready, and he was back in Triple-A a month later. When the season was over, the Padres surprised Lee by dealing him to the Florida Marlins, the defending World Series champions, in exchange for starter Kevin Brown.

The move gave Lee, still just 22 years old, an opportunity to play every day at first base. He showed his power with 17 home runs, but was often overmatched at the plate, as his .233 average attested. The following season he was demoted to the minors and batted just .206 during his call-ups. The Marlins had patience with Lee, however, and their faith paid off. In 2000, Lee's breakout season, he upped his average to .278 and pounded

$ 24.95
GATE 55
SECTION UPPER
SEAT CC8
P2ZO555
27AUG08

CAREER HIGHLIGHTS

- stole 81 bases between 2002 and 2007, more than any other first baseman

- led the NL in slugging (.662) and total bases (393) in 2005 while also winning his second Gold Glove

- selected to the NL All-Star Team in 2005 and 2007

25 FIRST BASE

Derrek LEE

28 home runs. He then put up similar numbers in the next two seasons as the Marlins flirted with .500.

The 2003 campaign saw Florida come out of nowhere to grab the National League wild card spot, and Lee was a big contributor with his bat, glove and legs. He knocked 31 home runs on the year, and batted .341 with 20 RBIs in September as the Marlins made their late-season charge. He committed just five errors and won his first Gold Glove, and he even chipped in with 21 stolen bases, a rare feat for a first baseman. The Marlins had a magical playoff run that year, ousting the Giants, Cubs and Yankees to win their second World Series, but Lee was a non-factor, batting .208 in the postseason.

With a new ring on his finger, Lee's stock was high, and the Marlins took the opportunity to trade him to the Cubs for first baseman Hee-Seop Choi, who turned out to be a bust. (Coincidentally, Choi had been scouted in Korea by Lee's father.) By now Lee had become a bona fide slugger, but few could have expected what happened in 2005. Normally a slow starter, Lee had one of the most torrid first months in club history, batting .419 in April. He followed that with a .313 clip and nine homers in May, and then hit .400 in June. By the All-Star break, Cubs fans were talking Triple Crown as Lee had compiled a .378 average with 27 homers and

72 RBIs. Not surprisingly, Lee cooled off in the second half, though his final numbers were still magnificent. His .335 average was enough to win the batting crown, and he finished with 46 homers and 50 doubles. His surprisingly low RBI total (107) was proof that the statistic can be misleading: the batters ahead of Lee in the lineup had terrible OBPs, and his opportunities with men on base were far fewer than normal.

Lee was off to a quick start again in 2006, with three home runs in the first four games, but in the middle of April he broke his right wrist in a collision on the basepaths. It turned out to be a painful year on and off the field: Lee tried to come back too soon and reinjured the wrist, and then late in the season he learned that his young daughter would lose her vision in one eye due to a rare genetic disease. It was a miserable year for the Cubs, too, as they lost 96 games and finished last in the NL Central.

Everything changed for Lee and the Cubs in 2007. With his wrist healthy again, Lee regained his stroke, batting .317 with 22 home runs, and also nabbed his third Gold Glove. The team, meanwhile, picked up Ted Lilly and Alfonso Soriano and hired a new manager in Lou Piniella. The investments paid off with 85 wins, and the Cubs caught the upstart Milwaukee Brewers in the final weeks to capture the division title.

justin MORNEAU

33

Justin Morneau grew up in New Westminster, British Columbia, and like many other Canadian kids, he played hockey. But he also excelled at basketball and baseball, and it was the latter sport that held out hopes for a pro career. It helped that Justin's dad owned a sporting goods store with a batting cage, where the young athlete honed his left-handed stroke well enough to earn a spot on Canada's World Junior team in 1999, the year he was drafted by Minnesota.

The Twins recognized that Morneau had huge potential, and by 2003 he was thriving in Triple-A Rochester. That June, his manager called him aside and told him he had been called up to the Show. It turned out to be a cup of coffee — in 40 games, he hit .226 with four homers — but he got people talking. In one pinch-hit appearance against the Brewers on June 22, Morneau sent a 1–0 pitch into the center field scoreboard at Miller Park. Estimated at 460 feet, it was the longest blast ever hit in that stadium.

Morneau was back in Triple-A to start 2004, but the Twins recalled him again in May when first baseman Doug Mientkiewicz was sidelined. His 19 homers in 280 at-bats were enough to convince the team that he was ready for the big time, and Mientkiewicz was traded away. The Twins went on to win the division for the third year in a row, but they bowed out quickly against the Yankees. Justin had a couple of doubles in the four-game series, but he batted .235 in his first postseason for the overmatched Twins.

Morneau struggled in 2005, his first full campaign in the bigs, but he had some convincing excuses. He suffered a string of illnesses in the preseason (chicken pox, pneumonia and appendicitis), and when things got underway in April he was promptly beaned and missed two weeks with a concussion. In June he needed a cortisone shot in his elbow and slumped again. He wound up batting .239 on the year — including a miserable .201 against lefties — and his extra-base hits

(22 homers, 23 doubles) were only a shade more than the year before, despite almost twice as many plate appearances.

He began 2006 with a .208 average in April and was perilously close to returning to Triple-A to get his bearings. By June 1 he had improved to .240 with 10 home runs, but this was not the kind of performance the Twins expected from him. Manager Ron Gardenhire laid it all out for his young first baseman, questioning Morneau's maturity and dedication.

Whatever Gardenhire said, it worked: from June 8 to the end of the season, Morneau led the majors with a scorching .362 average. His huge second half allowed him to finish at .321, with 34 homers, 37 doubles, 130 RBIs and a .559 slugging percentage. His hot bat helped the Twins win 96 games and finish on top of the AL Central for

$ 24.95

GATE 11

SECTION FIELD

SEAT HH33

U4DS163 17OCT08

CAREER HIGHLIGHTS

- hit three home runs in one game on July 6, 2007
- represented Team Canada at the 2006 World Baseball Classic, batting .308 in three games
- his 130 RBIs in 2006 were the most by a Twin since Harmon Killebrew had 140 in 1969

33 FIRST BASE

Justin MORNEAU

the fourth time in five years, and Morneau was eager to get a second chance at the postseason. The club met Oakland in the ALDS this time, and he did all he could to key the offense, batting .417 (5-for-12) with two homers, but the Twins scored just seven runs in the three-game sweep. It was some consolation for Morneau that he was voted the league's Most Valuable Player that November. The choice surprised many, given that Morneau did not lead the league in any major offensive category.

Morneau set out in 2007 to prove that his MVP season was no fluke. Indeed, during the first four months, he looked like he might even surpass his production of the previous year: in late July he already had 28 home runs, putting him on pace to top 40. But he tanked in the final two months, and from August 1 onward he batted .222 with three homers, ending the season much the way he had begun the previous one. Overall, however, Morneau's 2007 numbers were more than respectable. He is probably not going to hit over .320 again, but if he can become more consistent, Morneau should remain a potent threat for years to come.

albert
PUJOLS

Many great hitters take time to reach their prime, but Albert Pujols arrived in the major leagues as a fully formed superstar. With the possible exceptions of Ted Williams and Joe DiMaggio, there simply has never been another ballplayer whose first seven seasons have been so consistently magnificent.

Born in Santo Domingo, Dominican Republic, Pujols moved with his family to the US at age 16, eventually settling in Independence, Missouri. Scouts in St. Louis loved what they saw in this high-school prospect from across the state. Not only did Albert have rare physical talent, he showed uncanny instincts, thinking his way through each at-bat and always remaining aware of the game situation while on base and in the field. Few other teams seemed to notice, however — when the Cardinals drafted him in 1999, he went 402nd overall.

Playing third base in his first pro season in 2000, Pujols stomped on the Class-A Midwest League and jumped to Triple-A at season's end. He attended the Cardinals' training camp the following spring, but was a long shot to make the team until Bobby Bonilla was injured and a spot opened in left field. Pujols then surprised everyone by batting .351 with 16 home runs in April and May. Determined to get his bat into the lineup every day, the Cards played him in left field, right field, third base and first base, making him the first player ever to start at least 30 games at four different positions in one season. The 21-year-old wound up leading the team in almost every offensive category as he finished at .329 with 37 homers, 47 doubles, 130 RBIs and 112 runs scored — unbelievable numbers for a rookie.

In his sophomore season, Pujols posted very similar numbers to those of his debut and finished a distant second to Barry Bonds in the MVP voting. In 2003 he was batting .391 on June 29 and looked like he might make a run at .400. Though Pujols finished well short at .359, he still had the highest average in the majors to go along with 43 homers, 51 doubles, 137 runs scored and a dizzying OPS of 1.106.

The Cardinals won the NL pennant in 2004, as Pujols' teammates Scott Rolen and Jim Edmonds joined him in producing huge offensive numbers. Now a full-time first baseman, Pujols upped his career high to 46 home runs and led the league in extra-base hits (99) and total bases (389). He also had his best postseason to date, batting .414, including 14-for-28 with four home runs to take MVP honors in the NLCS against Houston.

After being among the top four vote-getters in each of his first four seasons, Pujols finally won the MVP award in 2005. While batting .330 with 41 home runs, he led the majors in runs scored for the third straight year, the first person to accomplish that since Pete Rose. Facing the Astros in the NLCS again that year, Pujols came up in the ninth inning of Game 5 with the Cards trailing 4–2 and facing elimination. With two on and two out, he crushed an 0–1 pitch from Brad Lidge way over the left-field wall for a game-winning three-run homer. The exultant Redbirds lost the next day, however, and the dream would have to wait another year.

Pujols opened 2006 by hitting 14 home runs in April, and he would certainly have finished the season with more than 50 had he not missed most of June with a muscle strain. As it was, he belted a career-high 49 and just missed accomplishing the extraordinary feat of tallying more homers than strikeouts, as he whiffed just 50 times. After a solid performance in the first two postseason series that October, Pujols hit .200 in the Fall Classic, but the underdog Cards shocked everyone by knocking off the Detroit Tigers in five games.

It is the rare player that can hit .327 with 32 home runs and 103 RBIs and have it be labeled an off-year, but that was Pujols' fate in 2007. Though he battled a hamstring strain much of the year, the first baseman still managed to extend his record-smashing string of seven straight seasons with a .300-plus average, 30 home runs, 100 runs and 100 RBIs, which dates back to the start of his career.

$ 24.95
GATE 4
SECTION FIELD
SEAT JJ7
R4SD887
13SEPT08

CAREER HIGHLIGHTS

- leads all active players with a career slugging percentage of .620
- all-time leader among right-handed batters with a 1.040 OPS
- only player to start his career with five 30-homer seasons, and the fourth to begin with seven 100-RBI campaigns

5 FIRST BASE

Albert PUJOLS

hanley
RAMIREZ

When Hanley Ramirez signed with the Boston Red Sox in the summer of 2000, the 16-year-old shortstop from the Dominican Republic was a big step closer to his dream. His fellow countryman Pedro Martinez was in the middle of his third Cy Young–winning season with the Bosox, and the teenager hoped to one day anchor the infield behind his hero.

Ramirez quickly became one of Boston's hottest prospects. He hit for average and ran like a deer, and by 2004 he was batting well over .300 in Double-A with a dozen steals in 32 games. But before the 2005 season opened, the Sox acquired All-Star shortstop Edgar Renteria and Ramirez wondered whether he figured into Boston's plans. He was called up that September, but had just two at-bats, striking out both times. In November the club traded Ramirez to the Florida Marlins in a deal to acquire pitcher Josh Beckett and third baseman Mike Lowell.

After an impressive spring training, Ramirez was the Marlins' Opening Day shortstop and leadoff man in 2006. He made an immediate impact, hitting safely in his first eight games and posting a .379 OBP and seven stolen bases in April. He also showed he had some pop in his bat: on April 18 he led off with his first big-league home run, and an inning later he launched his second. Ramirez slumped badly in June and much of July, but finished with a bang. In September alone he swatted 43 hits, including 21 for extra bases, and when the season was over Ramirez topped all NL rookies in batting average (.292), hits (185), doubles (46), runs (119) and stolen bases (51). The league boasted a number of other fine freshman in 2006 — including his double-play partner, second baseman Dan Uggla, who had 27 home runs — but the shortstop's hot streak in the final month swayed the vote, and Ramirez won Rookie of the Year honors.

It is rare for a first-year phenom to follow up with an even better sophomore season, but Ramirez did exactly that, and he wasted no time getting started. His OPS in April was 1.087 and he continued his tear throughout the first half. During a game against the Dodgers on July 6, Ramirez demonstrated how he can beat a team with his bat and his legs: he led off with a homer, added another in the seventh and then squeezed home the winning run in the 10th inning with a bunt single. At the break he was hitting .331 with 14 home runs, 70 runs scored and 27 stolen bases, yet somehow he was left off the NL All-Star Team. Ramirez's second-half performance was almost identical, and he challenged for the batting title, finishing at .332. His 212 hits included 29 homers and 48 doubles, and his 359 total bases were third-best in the league. Incredibly, he accomplished all of this despite nagging pain from a partially dislocated shoulder he suffered in July.

Ramirez's combination of power and speed reminds many fans of Alfonso Soriano during his best years; in fact, the Marlins' shortstop may soon join the Cubs' veteran outfielder in the exclusive 40–40 club. The only problem this presents for the Marlins is where to place him in the batting order. His .386 OBP and 51 steals in 2007 were the basic tools of a leadoff man, but when a player slugs .562 you want him coming up with men on base, not leading off games and batting after the pitcher. Ramirez started the season at the top of the order, then batted third for much of May and June before returning to the number-one slot by the end of the year.

The trade that sent Ramirez to Florida may appear to have favored Boston: Beckett was the majors' only 20-game winner in 2007, and Lowell's outstanding season helped the Red Sox win the World Series, while the Marlins finished dead-last in the NL East. But the Fish are loaded to the gills with young talent, and they should return to contention in the near future with Hanley Ramirez at the vanguard.

CAREER HIGHLIGHTS

- first National League rookie to collect more than 110 runs and 50 stolen bases (2006)

- hit seven leadoff homers in 2006, setting an NL record for rookies

- was one home run shy of becoming the third player in MLB history with 30 homers and 50 stolen bases in the same season (2007)

2 SHORTSTOP

Hanley RAMIREZ

jose REYES

During the final days of the 2007 season, as the New York Mets completed the worst collapse in MLB history by blowing a seven-game lead with 17 left to play, the boo birds targeted Jose Reyes. The shortstop batted a paltry .205 in September and failed to swipe a single base in his final 15 matches. Even more disturbing was his seeming lack of hustle, a problem that dated back to July 6. Three days before Reyes started his first All-Star Game, he hit a roller up the line that he thought was foul. It wasn't, and Reyes stood in the batter's box as the third baseman jogged slowly across the diamond to retire him and end the inning. Manager Willie Randolph immediately pulled Reyes out of the game, insisting that rookie mistakes were not acceptable from a player in his fifth season, even if he was still 24 years old.

Jose Reyes was born in Villa Gonzalez in the Dominican Republic, where Mets scouts spotted him while he was in high school. He signed at 16 years old and played Rookie-level ball for the Mets' affiliate in Kingsport, Tennessee, where the natural right-handed batter worked hard at developing his switch-hitting. The following year he jumped to Class-A, where he was co-winner of the team's MVP award despite being the youngest player in the league. In 2002 Reyes played in the All-Star Futures Game, which showcases the best minor-league talent. His three-run triple earned him the game's MVP award and put him squarely in the media spotlight. Although he was only

19, Reyes seemed big-league bound.

He got his opportunity the following June, when Mets shortstop Rey Sanchez went down with an injury. Reyes made his debut a day before his 20th birthday and went 2-for-4 with a double and two runs scored. He batted .205 that first month, but he made his hits count: he hit a grand slam in a game against Anaheim, and three days later drove in four more with a double and triple. The youngster who was called upon to plug a temporary hole wound up with 15 RBIs in his first 20 games. Convinced that Reyes was the real deal, the Mets shipped the aging Sanchez to Seattle in late July. The rookie continued to impress, and on August 27 he became the youngest player to hit a home run from each side of the plate in the same game. But his season ended early when he tore a ligament in his ankle trying to break up a double play. He was hitting .307 when the injury took him out of the lineup.

Before the 2004 campaign, the Mets acquired Kazuo Matsui from Japan, and the high-profile import was installed at shortstop. That shifted Reyes to second base, a position he had never played before. As it turned out, Reyes was injured for much of the year, and in

2005 the Mets moved the disappointing Matsui to second and reinstalled Reyes at short. Batting atop the order, he collected 190 hits and stole 60 bases, fine numbers for a leadoff man, but his OBP of .300 would have to improve if he was going to continue in that role.

Reyes evolved into a much more patient hitter in 2006. With coaching from the great Rickey Henderson, Reyes drew twice as many bases on balls, upping his OBP to .354. He also surprised everyone with his power, belting 19 home runs after hitting just 27 in his entire pro career to that point. Reyes had a particularly strong June, batting .373 with 17 extra-base hits, propelling him to a starting spot on the All-Star Team, though he was unable to play because of an injury. He finished the year at .300 with 122 runs scored and became the first Met to post back-to-back seasons with 60 steals.

Reyes came out swinging, walking and running in 2007. His home run total was down, but his job on the team was not to hit the ball out of the park. Instead, he concentrated on getting to first base, upping his OBP to .354, and then quickly moving on to second with his thievery. His 78 stolen bases set a franchise record and was the highest total in the majors since 1988. As a supremely talented player who responds well to coaching, Reyes is well on his way to becoming the finest shortstop of his generation.

$ 24.95
GATE 22
SECTION CLUB
SEAT H7
P4TT376
90CT08

CAREER HIGHLIGHTS

- three-time National League leader in stolen bases (2005–07)
- tops in the NL in triples in 2005 and 2006, with 17 in each season
- selected to the All-Star Game in 2006 and 2007

7 SHORTSTOP

Jose REYES

alex RODRIGUEZ

NEW YORK YANKEES ◆ AL East

Alex Rodriguez's list of achievements is dizzying: five AL home run titles, 11 All-Star selections, nine Silver Sluggers and three MVP awards. There is no doubt that he is one of the greatest players of all-time — and he was only 32 on Opening Day, 2008. If he stays healthy, he will no doubt take a run at some of the most hallowed records in baseball.

Rodriguez was born in New York City, though his parents moved back to their native Dominican Republic when he was four. They later returned to the States and settled in Miami, where Alex enrolled at Westminster Christian, a private high school with one of the best baseball teams in the country. The top prospect in the 1993 draft, he was selected first overall by the Seattle Mariners. A-Rod played his first full season at shortstop in 1996 and had a year like no one had ever seen from a 20-year-old. He won the batting title with a .358 average and socked 36 home runs. His 141 runs scored, 91 extra-base hits and .631 slugging percentage were all records for shortstops.

Rodriguez passed the 40-homer plateau each season from 1998 to 2000, and in the first of those years he added 46 steals to become the third 40–40 player in history. Not since Ernie Banks had a shortstop displayed the kind of power A-Rod exhibited, and it made him the hottest free agent on the market in the winter of 2001. Rodriguez had played five playoff series with the Mariners, but had never reached the World Series, and many thought he would try to sign with a contender. Instead, he followed the money: the Texas Rangers offered him $252 million over 10 years, the largest contract in sports history at that time.

Rodriguez was simply fantastic during his three years in Arlington, posting seasons of 52, 57 and 47 home runs. He won two Gold Gloves and his first MVP award. But despite his heroics, the Rangers finished at least 25 games back each year. Though many fans felt he got what he deserved, Rodriguez was fed up

and wanted out of Texas. But who would take on his gargantuan salary? Eventually the Yankees agreed to send Alfonso Soriano to the Rangers if Texas would continue to cover part of A-Rod's paycheck. New York now had two of the greatest players in the game in Rodriguez and Derek Jeter — unfortunately, both were shortstops. The newcomer was well aware that no one was going to replace the beloved Jeter, however, so Rodriguez willingly moved to third base.

The newest Yankee quickly learned how things worked in New York. It didn't matter that Rodriguez hit 36 home runs during his first year in pinstripes, or that he followed that up in 2005 with his second MVP award, batting .321 with 48 homers and 130 RBIs. What mattered was that he went 2-for-17 in the final four games of the 2004 ALCS against the arch-rival Red Sox, allowing Boston to storm back from a three-game deficit. The next year against the Angels in the ALDS he was 2-for-15. And in the 2006 playoffs he managed one single in 14 at-bats against the Tigers. Some fans in New York dealt him the worst insult they knew, saying A-Rod wasn't a real Yankee.

The Yankees waited until the second half to get going in 2007, but A-Rod was way ahead of them: he pounded 14 home runs in the first 18 games and went on to have a career year, even by his lofty standards. He reached the 50-homer plateau for the third time and set personal bests with 156 RBIs and a .645 slugging percentage. He was an easy choice for his third MVP award. But his playoff story was the same: though Rodriguez managed a solo homer in Game 4 of the ALDS against Cleveland, he was hitless with men on base, and the Yankees bowed out in four games. Their early exit, of course, could not be laid exclusively at his feet: Jeter (.176 in the series), Jorge Posada (.133), Hideki Matsui (.182) and Chien-Ming Wang (12 runs surrendered in two starts) played a large part. But when Yankee fans look for someone to blame, A-Rod is inevitably the lighting rod.

Rodriguez shocked the baseball world at season's end when he elected not exercise his option to rejoin the Yankees in 2008. A few weeks later, he announced that he would be returning after all, and he signed a 10-year, $275-million dollar deal. He does, after all, still have some unfinished business in New York.

$ 24.95
GATE
SECTION 54
FIELD
SEAT
HH52
S5CC675
19MAY08

CAREER HIGHLIGHTS

- leads all players in home runs (454) and runs scored (1,241) over the past decade (1998–07)

- owns MLB single-season records for home runs by a shortstop (57 in 2002) and by a third baseman (54 in 2007)

- youngest player to reach 500 career home runs (32 years, 8 days)

13 THIRD BASE

Alex RODRIGUEZ

scott
ROLEN

Scott Rolen came full circle during his first decade in the majors. As a rookie with the Philadelphia Phillies in 1997, he won over teammates and fans with his big bat, his even bigger glove, and his maturity, intelligence and leadership abilities. The young star appeared to be a franchise player like another Phillies third baseman named Mike Schmidt, who entered Cooperstown the year before Rolen broke into the bigs. But the team was in the midst of seven straight sub-.500 seasons, and Rolen's frustration boiled over. He feuded with manager Larry Bowa, and was sent packing midseason in 2002. As a member of the St. Louis Cardinals, however, he again assumed a leadership role. Joining superstars like Albert Pujols, Jim Edmonds and Chris Carpenter, Rolen became a four-time All-Star and a key player in the Cardinals' two National League pennants.

The Phillies drafted Rolen in 1993. He was a late-season call-up three years later, and then made a tremendous debut in 1997. His .283 average, 21 home runs (tops on his club) and 92 RBIs led all first-year National Leaguers and made him the unanimous choice as Rookie of the Year, despite playing on a terrible team that went 68–94. He followed with a brilliant sophomore campaign, becoming just the second Phillie to reach 40 doubles, 30 homers, 100 runs and 100 RBIs in the same season. In the field, Rolen was a magician, and at age 23 he was the youngest third baseman ever to win an NL Gold Glove. That kind of performance drew comparisons with his Hall of Fame predecessor, and while Rolen will never approach Mike Schmidt's home-run numbers, he may well be the better defensive player. At six-foot-four he covers enormous ground — he stops virtually anything hit down the line, yet he is still able to grab so many balls to his left that his shortstop can cheat toward second base. More than one baseball analyst has called him the greatest defensive third baseman ever.

Rolen posted another 100-RBI season in 2001, but then his relationship with Philadelphia unraveled.

He shocked the Phillies' management by turning down a big contract extension, had an on-field shouting match with Bowa in spring training, and was finally traded to the Cardinals 100 games into the 2002 season. Transported from last place to a division winner, Rolen got into his first postseason that year, but it ended early when an Arizona base runner collided with him in Game 2 of the NLDS. He watched from the bench as the Cards swept the Diamondbacks and then lost to the Giants in five games in the Championship Series.

Rolen's biggest year came in 2004, when he batted .314 with 34 home runs and 124 RBIs. With Pujols and Edmonds, he was part of the most fearsome three-four-five combination of any batting order in recent memory — all three finished in the top five in MVP voting — and the Cardinals won 105 games. Rolen was a dismal 0-for-12 in the Division Series. He redeemed himself by batting .310 with three home runs in the NLCS, including the winning blast in Game 7, but then went AWOL in the World Series, posting a miserable 0-for-15.

Injured for most of 2005, Rolen came back to help the Cardinals limp into the 2006 postseason despite their mediocre 83–78 record. He hit poorly in the first two series until singling in the ninth inning of Game 7 of the NLCS against the Mets, and then scored on Yadier Molina's improbable game-winning homer. In his second World Series, Rolen finally shook off his reputation as a guy who can't hit in October. He batted .421 with three doubles and a homer in 19 at-bats as the Cardinals bested the Tigers in five games to get Rolen his first ring.

Rolen ended his 2007 season early to undergo surgery. In January 2008, Rolen, unhappy with manager Tony La Russa, was sent to the Toronto Blue Jays for Troy Glaus. The Jays are confident that a change in uniform will spark a return to form for Rolen at the hot corner.

$ 24.95
GATE 16
SECTION CLUB
SEAT H22
T5HU776
29JULY08

CAREER HIGHLIGHTS

- won seven Gold Gloves at third base, behind only Brooks Robinson (16) and Mike Schmidt (10)

- has three seasons with 45 or more doubles (1998, 2003, 2006) and seven straight with 25 or more homers (1998–04)

- owns a .507 career slugging percentage, higher than George Brett (.487) and close to Eddie Matthews (.509), both Hall of Fame third basemen

27 THIRD BASE

Scott ROLEN

mark
TEIXEIRA

Growing up in Annapolis, Maryland, Mark Teixeira spent his Little League days in Baltimore Orioles territory, but his favorite player was Don Mattingly, the sweet-swinging Yankees first baseman. When Teixeira eventually made it to the big leagues as a first-sacker, he even wore Mattingly's number 23 on his Texas Rangers jersey. (He now wears number 24 in Atlanta.) Teixeira may never match Mattingly's lifetime batting average of .307, but he has already displayed more power with the stick and equally soft hands in the field.

The teenaged Teixeira was one of the hottest high-school players in the US, and the Boston Red Sox were courting him as the 1998 draft approached. The Bosox had led him to believe they were going to select him early, and when they waited until the ninth round Teixeira felt snubbed and chose not to sign. Instead, he enroled at Georgia Tech, where he had a marvelous college career, batting .409 with 36 homers and 165 RBIs over three seasons. In his sophomore year, the young switch hitter topped .400 from each side of the plate, and when he was eligible for the draft again in 2001, Teixeira went in the first round, chosen fifth overall by the Rangers.

Teixeira had a good spring training in 2003 and became a full-timer that year, playing mostly at first, but also a bit of third and outfield. He had a fine rookie season, leading all major-league freshmen with 26 home runs and 60 extra-base hits. He struggled against right-handed pitchers, however, hitting 53 points lower from the left side. He also generated a lot of breeze with his strikeouts, but it was clear that the Rangers had a future star on their hands.

Unable to find his groove early in 2004, Teixeira took until June to heat up, but once he did, he pounded the ball to the tune of 38 homers. He also racked up 112 RBIs and 101 runs scored to win a Silver Slugger in just his second season. On August 17 against Cleveland, Teixeira struck out his first time up, and then doubled, homered, tripled and singled in his next four at-bats to become just the second Ranger to hit for the cycle. Only two other switch hitters in MLB history had accomplished the feat with a pair of hits from each side of the plate.

Teixeira put together an MVP-type season in 2005. Playing on a powerful Rangers club that led the AL in long balls, he swatted 43 homers, drove in 144 runs, topped the league in total bases, and capped it all with a .301 average. He also led AL first basemen in total chances while making only three errors for a fielding percentage of .998. While Teixeira did not win the league's top award that fall, his mantle sparkled with two precious metals as he copped his second straight Silver Slugger and his first Gold Glove.

Falling into a pattern of slow starts, Teixeira finished the first half of 2006 with just nine home runs. But in the first game after the All-Star break, the big first baseman went yard three times in Baltimore, then pounded 21 more home runs before the year was out to finish with 33. He also added a career-high 45 doubles and 110 RBIs, the third straight season he had driven in 100 or more. Nineteen of those RBIs were game winners to lead the AL in that department.

Just before the trading deadline in July 2007, Teixeira was part of the season's biggest swap. The Rangers dealt him to the Atlanta Braves in exchange for several young prospects, most notably Jarrod Saltalamacchia. Back in the state where he had excelled during his college years, Teixeira had quite a homecoming: in August he batted .315 with a .640 slugging percentage, notching 10 homers and 32 RBIs to win NL Player of the Month. The Braves missed the postseason for the second straight year in 2007, but with Teixeira's bat in the lineup, the team may be poised to begin another long run of division titles.

$ 24.95
GATE 45
SECTION UPPER
SEAT 06
P5SR185
14AUG08

CAREER HIGHLIGHTS

- one of only four players in history to tally 140 or more home runs in his first four seasons

- established a single-season record for RBIs by a switch hitter with 144 (2005)

- two-time Silver Slugger winner (2004–05) and two-time Gold Glover (2005–06)

24 FIRST BASE

Mark TEIXEIRA

miguel
TEJADA

HOUSTON ASTROS ◆ NL Central

CAREER HIGHLIGHTS

- played 1,152 consecutive games between 2000 and 2007, the fifth-longest streak in MLB history

- owns 255 career home runs as a shortstop, behind only Cal Ripken and Alex Rodriguez on the AL's all-time list

- selected to four All-Star Teams (2002, 2004–06)

10 SHORTSTOP

Miguel TEJADA

Like many boys growing up in the Dominican Republic, Miguel Tejada idolized the major-league shortstops that hailed from his island country. His favorite was Alfredo Griffin, who was AL Rookie of the Year with the Blue Jays in 1979 and later patrolled the infield for the Athletics and Dodgers. But Tejada could not have turned out more different from his hero. The slick-fielding, light-hitting Griffin tallied 24 home runs over 18 seasons. Tejada, meanwhile, is an occasionally brilliant, but frustratingly inconsistent fielder who may someday take a run at the record for career home runs by a shortstop.

A stocky five-foot-nine and 215 pounds, Tejada doesn't even look like a middle infielder. But his bat looked good enough to attract the attention of Juan Marichal, the great Dominican pitcher who had six 20-win seasons in the 1960s. Marichal was a scout with Oakland in the early 1990s, and he convinced Tejada to sign with A's in 1993. Within three years he was the organization's top prospect, and after a big campaign in Double-A in 1997 (22 homers, 97 RBIs), the 21-year-old Tejada won a spot on the big club the following year.

The A's had a few concerns about their young slugger-to-be. He could drive the ball, that was for sure, but he lacked the discipline to lay off pitches out of the strike zone. (Tejada and others who grew up poor in the Dominican Republic often justify their free-swinging ways by pointing out that "you can't *walk* off the island.") Early on, he also had trouble with right-handed pitchers: in his first three seasons he batted a combined .240 off righties.

As 2000 dawned, Tejada was 23 and loaded with potential, and it would prove to be a breakout year for both the shortstop and his club. Tejada batted .275 with 30 homers and knocked in 115 runs as the Athletics won the AL West for the first time in eight years. The A's went on to make the playoffs in the next three seasons as well, but they failed to get past the Division Series every year, losing in five games each time. Tejada hit .350 against the Yankees in the first of those series, but overall he posted a dismal OBP of .242 in his 20 postseason games with Oakland.

In 2002, with Jason Giambi gone, the A's looked to Tejada to anchor the offense, and he came through in a big way. He had his first 200-hit season, pushed his average to .308, whacked a career-high 34 home runs (his third straight season with 30 or more), slugged .508 and drove in 131 runs to win AL MVP honors over Alex Rodriguez. The Texas shortstop also had a monster year for the last-place Rangers, but Tejada consistently came up big when the A's put together a magical 20-game win streak and steamrolled their way to a division title. He secured the 18th of those victories on September 1 with

a walk-off three-run homer (his second dinger of the game) to overcome a 5–4 Twins lead. The next night, as the A's tried to make it 19 in a row, they spotted the Royals a 5–0 lead, then fought back to make it 6–6. In the bottom of the ninth, Tejada lined a single to center to chase home the winning run.

Tejada became a free agent after the 2003 season, and it was clear that the A's would not be able to afford him. He accepted a six-year, $72-million offer from the Baltimore Orioles, and in his first season with the O's, he batted .311, belted 34 homers and drove in a dizzying 150 runs, the second highest total ever posted by a shortstop. Although he has never come close to repeating those numbers, the hitter-friendly dimensions of Camden Yards turned Tejada into a consistent .300 hitter, and in 2006 he hit a career-best .330 (including .357 at home) and logged his sixth 100-RBI season.

For the first time in his career, Tejada endured a spell on the disabled list in 2007 and had a disappointing campaign, with just 18 home runs. His name repeatedly came up in trade rumors, and in the offseason the O's dealt him to the Houston Astros for five players they hope will help retool the Baltimore franchise. The move will send Tejada to the National League for the first time in his career, where he will get to work on a whole new crop of unsuspecting pitchers.

chase UTLEY

26

PHILADELPHIA PHILLIES ◆ NL East

Not many second basemen can pound 25 or 30 home runs and collect 100 RBIs in the heart of a batting order. Ryne Sandberg and Joe Morgan did it, and they ended up in the Hall of Fame. Jeff Kent did it in his prime as well, and he's likely to follow Sandberg and Morgan into Cooperstown. Chase Utley is a long way from having a plaque etched with his name, but his first three seasons have been among the best ever by a young second-sacker.

Born in Pasadena, California, Utley accepted a baseball scholarship from UCLA, where he batted .342 with 174 RBIs over three seasons. In his junior year, he was named Outstanding Player of the NCAA Regionals and got noticed by the Philadelphia Phillies, who took him in the first round of the 2001 draft. By 2002 he had made the jump to Triple-A and was hopeful of cracking the big-league squad the following year.

Utley had a good spring training in 2003 and backed into a spot on the Opening Day roster, but the Phillies soon sent him back to Triple-A so he could get more playing time. Recalled in late April, he made an impression in his third major-league at-bat, launching a grand slam in a 9–1 win over the Rockies. The party didn't last, however, and Utley was back in the minors in May, where he spent the rest of 2003 and all of 2004 bouncing between the farm and the big club.

In 2005 the Phils decided to platoon Utley and Placido Polanco at second base, but by early June it was clear who the

future belonged to: Polanco was shipped to Detroit and Utley assumed the everyday role. That move was looking pretty good at the end of the season when Utley had compiled a .291 average and a slugging percentage of .540, with 39 doubles and 28 homers. He also drove in 105 runs to set a Phillies record for second basemen.

Utley was clearly itching to get the 2006 season underway, and he began the year early by participating in the World Baseball Classic, where he batted .385. While a number of MLB players took a pass on this international tournament, Utley was thrilled to have the opportunity to represent his country. Indeed, when the MLB season was over, he flew overseas to play in another tourney against a Japanese All-Star team. That's a lot of baseball in one year, but Utley thrived on the competition. A quiet player who shuns the limelight, he is an intense competitor whose coaches and teammates often remark on his fervent desire to win.

Sandwiched between these two extracurriculars, Utley put together an outstanding season in 2006. He batted .291 with 32 home runs, 40 doubles, 102 RBIs, and a league-leading 131 runs scored. From June 23 to August 3, he compiled a 35-game hit streak, tied for the tenth-longest in major-league history. Those heady numbers earned him a Silver Slugger and even a few MVP votes.

Utley might have had a shot at the MVP award in 2007 had he not missed a month with an injury. He was hitting .336 with 17 homers and 82 RBIs on July 26 when he had his right hand broken by a pitch. Utley was back sooner than expected — despite undergoing surgery and having a metal pin inserted — and he went 3-for-5 with a home run in his first game back. He finished the year with a robust .332 average, third best in the league.

A player who swings a bat like Utley would have a big-league job even if he was a defensive klutz, and for much of his career he was a question mark in the field. But he has worked extremely hard to improve his glove work and his throwing arm, and he's made vast improvements — in 2007 both his fielding percentage and his range were well above the league average. He's not yet the complete player that Ryne Sandberg was, but Chase Utley is heading in the right direction.

$ 24.95

GATE 16

SECTION FIELD

SEAT S60

E8VC128

1SEPT08

CAREER HIGHLIGHTS

- first Phillies player since 1932 to collect at least 200 hits and 30 home runs in the same season (2006)

- led all major-league second basemen in combined hits, runs, home runs and RBIs from 2005 through 2007

- his 97 home runs and 388 RBIs in 576 games are well ahead of Ryne Sandberg and Jeff Kent at the same point in their careers

26 SECOND BASE

Chase UTLEY

david WRIGHT

NEW YORK METS ◆ NL East

Shortly after David Wright debuted with the Mets midway through 2004, the cover of the *New York Post*'s sports section featured a photo of the 21-year-old third baseman under the headline "Great Wright Hope." At the time, the Mets were in the middle of their third consecutive losing season. Wright's quick evolution from prospect to proven hitter has been one of the big factors in the turnaround that helped the team win the division title in 2006 and almost win a second the following year.

Wright began his 2004 campaign in the Double-A Eastern League, where he batted .363 with 10 homers in 60 games before being promoted to Triple-A. On July 21 the Mets called up Wright when Ty Wigginton was injured, and that was that: he manned third base in every game for the rest of the year and has been a fixture at the hot corner ever since. Despite garnering just 263 at-bats that first year, Wright led NL freshmen with a .293 average and slugged .525 with 14 home runs. Not bad for a kid who had been given no chance of making the team in spring training.

The Mets had high hopes for 2005. They signed free agents Pedro Martinez and Carlos Beltran in the offseason, and the team's other hot prospect, Jose Reyes, was slated to be the everyday shortstop. In the end, it was Wright who turned out to be the dominant offensive player in the lineup. Showing that his rookie numbers were no fluke, he led the club with a .306 average, 42 doubles, 102 RBIs and an OPS of .911. His 27 home runs were 11 more than Beltran, whose salary was 36 times higher. Wright's discerning eye at the plate led to 72 walks, and he even swiped 17 bases. While he was unspectacular defensively — his 24 errors led the league — Wright did manage to turn one of the greatest plays of the season, when he ran down a blooper off the bat of Ryan Klesko and then dove headlong toward left field to barehand the ball. That kind of hustle and spirit was a welcome addition to a team that was struggling

to get back into contention. The Mets finished a distant third, but they won 83 games to finish with their best record since 2000.

Wright began the 2006 season with a huge first half. After slugging .585 in April, he had three walk-off RBIs in May, and then received NL Player of the Month honors in June after batting .327 with 10 home runs. During that month, Wright and his infield partner Reyes also shared Player of the Week honors as they helped the first-place Mets improve to 43–25. By the break, Wright had 20 homers and a franchise-record 74 RBIs. That earned him a trip to his first All-Star Game, where he finished second in the Home Run Derby to the hulking Ryan Howard. Not to be denied his own long-ball glory, Wright attacked a Kenny Rogers changeup in his first All-Star Game at-bat and launched it over the left field wall to knot the score at 1–1. After that impressive showing, Wright's power abandoned him in the second half of 2006 — he was homerless from July 29 to August 29, and again from September 1 to 22. The Mets did not seem worried, though: in the middle of that first drought, they agreed to a six-year contract extension worth $55 million. The team went on to win the division and sweep the Dodgers in the NLDS.

When Wright opened the 2007 season by batting .244 without a single home run in April, that contract was looking like a big mistake. But he turned everything around by socking eight homers in May, six more in June, and soon erased any doubts about whether he really was a power hitter. Wright also surprised fans — and opposing pitchers and catchers — with his ability to steal despite only average speed. On August 30 he swiped his 30th bag of the year, and on September 16 he hit his 30th home run, becoming the third Met to join the 30–30 club. He picked up the Silver Slugger and, somewhat controversially, won his first Gold Glove at third base. He placed fourth in the MVP voting, a result that might have been even better if the Mets had not collapsed in the final week of the season.

dmitri
YOUNG

WASHINGTON NATIONALS ◆ NL East

When Dmitri Young walked to the plate as a pinch hitter in the ninth inning of the 2007 All-Star Game, he was thinking about a comeback. With his National League squad trailing 5–2 and down to their final out, Young grounded a base hit up the middle, and then scored when Alfonso Soriano homered to cut the lead to one. The All-Star rally came up short that night, as the NL lost the game 5–4. But for Young, the personal comeback was complete.

In September of 2006 Dmitri Young's baseball career looked to be over. Playing in his fifth season with the Detroit Tigers, he was in the worst shape of his life and had played fewer than 50 games. That spring he had pleaded guilty to domestic violence after assaulting a young woman in a Michigan hotel, and had admitted to a long battle with alcoholism. On September 5 he fell asleep in the clubhouse during a rain delay, and the fed-up Tigers released him the next day. It was a tragic fall for a player who had once been among the most positive, likeable players when the Tigers were a terrible team. Now Detroit was heading to the World Series, and Young wouldn't be part of it.

In November, things got even worse. Young checked into hospital after becoming violently ill and learned that he had diabetes. His blood sugar was so high and the symptoms so bad that Young thought he would die. It was hard to imagine he would ever return to the major leagues.

Young's father had been a navy pilot who flew an F-14 in Vietnam, and he was a harsh disciplinarian who drove his boys hard. (Dmitri's brother Delmon, 12 years younger, also made it to the majors with the Tampa Bay Devil Rays in 2006.) Dmitri's dad would take him to the batting cage and insist he take 200 swings a day. The regimen not only honed his swing, but it also turned him into a switch hitter: when his arms got tired, he turned around and hit from the other side of the plate.

Young was drafted fourth overall in 1991, and though his path to the majors was longer than expected, he batted .310 with 14 home runs and 48 doubles for the Cincinnati Reds in 1998, his first full year in the bigs. He went on to have three more .300-plus campaigns with the Reds and established himself not only as a consistently fine hitter, but also as a fun-loving guy with a ready smile who was popular with teammates, coaches and the front office. After the 2001 campaign, Young was traded to Detroit, who had just endured eight consecutive losing seasons. He sat out most of 2002 due to injury, then became a bright spot on the Tigers, particularly in 2003, when he led the club with a .297 average and 29 home runs as they posted one of the worst records in major-league history.

In the spring of 2007 the player who fans nicknamed "Da Meat Hook" was out of a job. Then he got an unexpected phone call from Jim Bowden, the general manager of the Washington Nationals, who had been the Reds' boss during Young's tenure. Bowden and the Nats were willing to give Young a chance in spring training. Despite showing up in poor physical condition, he earned a spot as the everyday first baseman and celebrated by smacking two doubles on Opening Day. He soon cooled off, however, and by the end of April he was batting a mere .253. But before anyone could say "washout," Young went on the greatest tear of his career. He was 23-for-58 (.397) in May, then followed with a .377 clip in June and finished the first half sporting a .339 average. When the All-Star lineups were announced, Young learned that he would be the Nationals' sole representative at the Midsummer Classic.

Another strong month in August (.373 with a .614 slugging percentage) helped Young finish the season batting .320 (a career high), with 13 home runs, 38 doubles and 74 RBIs as the Nationals' cleanup hitter — a fitting role for a player who cleaned up his life in 2007.

michael YOUNG

In any other era, Michael Young might have been the best all-around shortstop in baseball. He has posted five straight seasons (one as a second baseman) with a .300 average and at least 200 hits, and he's won a batting title. He's one of the game's best clutch performers, hitting over .380 with runners in scoring position from 2005 to 2007. He has a solid glove and a cannon of an arm. But Young has so far played his whole career on a bad team where he's been overshadowed by giants in the infield, including Alex Rodriguez, Rafael Palmeiro, Alfonso Soriano and Mark Teixeira.

Young was drafted by the Baltimore Orioles in 1994, but chose college over professional baseball. Three years later, Toronto selected him in the draft, but then dealt him away in what turned out to be one of the Blue Jays' worst trades of the decade. Pinning their hopes on middle infielders Cesar Izturis and Felipe Lopez, the Jays offered Young to the Texas Rangers in exchange for pitcher Esteban Loiza in July 2000. Izturis and Lopez went on to become journeyman .250 hitters, while Loiza went 25–28 in two-and-a-half unremarkable seasons in Toronto. Michael Young, meanwhile, blossomed into a superstar.

The Rangers slotted Young at second base to start 2001, and the rookie had a decent first campaign. But no one noticed a .249 hitter on a team that finished

$ 24.95

GATE **7**

SECTION **FIELD**

SEAT **T5**

A2NB265

16OCT08

CAREER HIGHLIGHTS

- fastest Texas Ranger to reach 1,000 hits (827 games)
- owns a lifetime .343 average with runners in scoring position, leading the AL in that category in 2005 and 2006
- named to four straight All-Star Teams (2004–07)

10 SHORTSTOP

Michael YOUNG

an astounding 43 games off the pace, especially since he was flanked by Rodriguez (52 homers) at shortstop and Palmeiro (47 homers) at first base. The next season Young improved slightly to .262, while A-Rod and Palmeiro again pounded the ball in vain on a club with a terrible pitching staff.

Young established himself as a hitter in 2003. He started the season near the bottom of the order, but when his average hovered around .330 in June, he moved to the leadoff spot for the rest of the year. Young went on to stroke 204 hits, including 33 doubles and 14 home runs, finishing with a .306 average.

After his breakout season, the Rangers asked Young to surrender his second base spot to Soriano, who arrived in the deal that sent A-Rod to the Yankees. He accepted the arrangement without complaint and took his place at shortstop in what turned out to be a powerhouse infield. Young batted .313 with 216 hits and upped his home run total to 22, joining Teixeira, Soriano and third baseman Hank Blalock as the first quartet of infielders since 1940 to surpass 20 homers each. The Rangers actually turned themselves into contenders in 2004, finishing only two games back in the wild card race.

In 2005 Young moved to the number-two slot in the batting order to make more effective use of his power. The strategy worked, as Young smacked 40 doubles and 24 homers. He also drove in 91 runs by making the most of his opportunities: he batted .368 with runners in scoring position, best in the AL, upping that to .450 when there were two outs. Overall he tallied a major-league-high 221 hits and won his first batting crown with a .331 average. Young was the picture of consistency that year, never going three consecutive games without a hit.

When Young collected 217 safeties in 2006, he joined only three other players who had eclipsed the 200-hit mark four years in a row since 1940. While his homer total slipped to 14, he sprayed the field with 52 doubles and again led the AL in hitting with runners in scoring position with a scorching .412 average. That outstanding clutch hitting enabled him to drive in 103 runs, second only to Teixeira on the club. Young's power dropped off again in 2007, when he collected just nine homers, but he continued to rack up the hits. Stuck on 197 entering the second-last game, he went 3-for-5 to reach the 200-hit plateau for a fifth straight year.

Michael Young has never won a Gold Glove, but he has won praise for his sure-handedness: in 2006, he ranked first in the league in double plays and assists per nine innings, and his .981 fielding percentage was second in the loop. A *Baseball America* poll of managers also rated his arm the strongest in the AL. With the big mashers now gone from the Texas infield, Young should emerge from the shadows and be recognized for his exceptional skills.

BACKSTOPS

victor
MARTINEZ

Victor Martinez did not take it well when the Cleveland Indians decided to make him a catcher at age 18. Martinez had grown up in Venezuela and fancied himself a shortstop like his hero, Ozzie Guillen. Now his club wanted him to don a suit of armor, squat behind the plate and take foul tips off his body. At first Martinez thought the team was setting him up to fail; in reality, they were looking for a way to get him into a big-league lineup. Martinez, a switch hitter with line-drive power and a habit of delivering in the clutch, had plenty of promise with the bat, but his lack of speed meant there was no way he was going to be a major-league shortstop.

To his credit, Martinez worked hard to learn his new position, and his coaches saw that he had the intelligence and keen instincts needed to call a game. But his value was primarily as a hitter: in 2001 he batted .329 at Class-A, and then improved to .336 in Double-A the next year, winning the batting title and league MVP both seasons. The Indians called him up for a look in September 2002, and in training camp the following spring he caught the eye of batting coach Eddie Murray, one of the greatest switch hitters of all time. Murray pegged the young slugger for future stardom.

After starting the 2003 season batting .328 in Triple-A, the Indians summoned Martinez for good in late June. For the rest of the season he shared duties with Josh Bard, another young switch-hitting catcher, and batted a respectable .289 in 49 games. When Bard missed almost all of 2004 with an injury, Martinez took over the everyday job and promptly stamped his name on it: at the break he was batting .290 with a dozen home runs and was selected to the All-Star Team. On July 16 Martinez had a career game at the plate, knocking three home runs and adding two singles, a walk and seven RBIs in an 18–6 rout of the Seattle Mariners. He kept up the pace throughout the second half and finished with 23 home runs and 108 RBIs,

leading all major-league catchers in both categories and tying Ivan Rodriguez for the Silver Slugger Award.

Martinez's big 2004 season earned him a reputation as a patient contact hitter — he drew 60 walks and fanned only 69 times — and as a reliable batter in the clutch. He batted .319 with men on base (his lifetime average in that situation is .314) and his coaches and teammates also praised his work ethic and his leadership qualities around the clubhouse. Defensively, his good hands and agility help him block pitches in the dirt, though the knock against him has always been his mediocre arm strength. (In recent years the Indians have experimented with him at first base, a position he fields well.)

During the spring of 2005, the Indians signed Martinez to a five-year deal that will pay him $15 million, and for the first two months of the season the Indians' brass must have been wringing their hands over the deal. On June 9 Martinez was batting .209 and the Tribe was 11½ games out of first place in the Central with a 28–30 record. Everything changed after the break, as Cleveland went 38–18 from August onward, led by the red-hot bat of their catcher. Martinez batted

CAREER HIGHLIGHTS

$ 24.95
GATE 2
SECTION FIELD
SEAT G14
S5KP167
14JULY08

- only catcher to hit over .300 in each season from 2005 to 2007
- led all MLB catchers in RBIs in 2004, 2005 and 2007
- selected to the AL All-Star Team in 2004 and 2007

41 CATCHER
Victor MARTINEZ

.380 (best in the majors) and slugged .578 in the second half. He ended the season with a .305 average, 20 home runs and 80 RBIs. The Indians took a serious charge at the White Sox for the AL Central crown, but were unable to catch the eventual World Series champs.

Martinez upped his average to a career-best .316 in 2006 and drove in 93 runs. Usually a slow starter, he bucked the trend by hitting .395 in April, reaching base safely in every game that month. He had a terrible May, going 15-for-91 (.165) with no home runs, but that was the only stain on an otherwise outstanding campaign that included a personal-best .391 OBP. The Indians, however, followed up their 93-win season of 2005 with a disappointing fourth-place finish.

When the Tribe turned things around in 2007, it was Martinez who led the offense. Batting cleanup behind Travis Hafner, the catcher led his team in almost every category: average (.301), home runs (25), RBIs (114), slugging (.505) and OPS (.879). He also threw out 30 percent of runners who tried to steal against him, double his rate of 2006. Meanwhile, the Indians put together the best record in baseball and Martinez continued his hot hitting in his first postseason, compiling a .318 average, knocking a home run in each series and driving in seven runs in 11 games before being eliminated by the Red Sox.

joe MAUER

MINNESOTA TWINS ◆ AL Central

The Minnesota Twins' catcher is no ordinary Joe —
indeed, there simply has never been another major-
league backstop like Joe Mauer. To begin with, his body
appears all wrong for the position. Catchers repeatedly
squat, stand and squat again, motions that are suited to
a short, stocky build. Mauer, by contrast, is a towering
six-foot-five. And whereas most catchers are plodders
on the basepaths, Mauer can swipe a dozen bags a year.
Finally, when it comes to hitting, managers are usually
happy if their backstop can hit .260 with decent power.
Joe Mauer, meanwhile, hits fewer home runs than most
second basemen, but sports a career average of .313,
and in 2006 he became the only catcher ever to win an
American League batting crown.

Mauer is a hometown hero in Minneapolis–St. Paul.
He grew up just a few miles from the Metrodome and
attended the same high school as Hall of Famer Paul
Molitor. His accomplishments in high school became
legendary in Minnesota: he was twice named to the
All-State basketball team, and in 2001 he was the first
player ever to be named by *USA Today* as the country's
best high school player in both baseball and football.
His buzz was so loud when the draft rolled around that
the Minnesota Twins grabbed him with the first overall
pick, passing over the equally promising Mark Prior.

In 2003 Mauer batted .338 in the minors and the
Twins decided that he was ready to be their starting
catcher the following season, even though he would still
be a week shy of his 21st birthday on Opening Day. The
club's confidence in Mauer was so great that they traded
A.J. Pierzynski — a .300 hitter in both 2002 and 2003
— to the San Francisco Giants for pitchers Joe Nathan,
Francisco Liriano and Boof Bonser. (No disrespect to
Pierzynski, a two-time All-Star, but that deal now looks
awfully lopsided.)

Mauer's much ballyhooed debut in 2004 featured a
terrifying moment. In his third big-league game, he was
chasing a foul popup when he suffered a torn meniscus

in his left knee. All of a sudden, Mauer's catching career looked as if it might be threatened before it had begun. He returned in June and played another six weeks, but when the injury did not heal properly, the Twins wisely pulled the plug on his season. Mauer was too young and too valuable to take chances with.

The knee appeared to be fine in 2005: Mauer caught 116 games and led the Twins starting nine with a .294 average (including .323 against righties), and added 13 steals in 14 attempts. He was outstanding defensively as well, using his athleticism to pounce on bunts and his rocket arm to toss out would-be thieves. A humble and low-key young man, it took him some time to be assertive with pitchers, especially superstars like Johan Santana. But eventually, as his confidence grew, he proved adept at calling for the right pitches in every game situation.

With hopes raised for 2006, Mauer hit .319 in the first month, upped that to .386 in May and then attacked the ball at a 42-for-93 clip in June to push his average to .378 by the All-Star break. A line drive hitter who uses the whole field, Mauer legged out 22 doubles and a whole lot of singles in the first half. By September he was still leading the league at .350, eight points ahead of Derek Jeter. The Yankees shortstop overtook him in the middle of the month, but Mauer surged in the final weeks to capture the batting title with a .347 mark. His 79 walks (21 of them intentional) gave him an OBP of .429, and he struck out a mere 54 times, about once in every nine plate appearances. It was one of the best offensive seasons ever by a young catcher, though it was marred by an early exit in the postseason at the hands of the Oakland A's. Mauer was 2-for-11 (.182) in the three-game sweep.

Mauer's 2007 season was disappointing on a number of levels. The Twins never took a serious run at the division, and the defending batting champ battled a strained quadricep muscle and a strained hamstring. Worst of all was that some of his teammates whispered to the press that he seemed unwilling to play through pain. Limited to 109 games, Mauer still managed to hit .293. No one believes that the sweet-swinging catcher is a one-year wonder — indeed, *Baseball Prospectus* projects that he'll bat .325 or better in each of the next four seasons. Still only 25 years old, this extraordinary Joe may well have another batting title in his future.

$ 24.95
GATE 25
SECTION FIELD
SEAT B28
18AUG08
F5TS298

CAREER HIGHLIGHTS

- posted a .347 average in 2006 to become the only AL catcher ever to win a batting title
- owns a career batting average of .313, highest among active catchers
- selected to the AL All-Star Team in 2006

7 CATCHER

Joe MAUER

brian MᶜCANN

ATLANTA BRAVES ◆ NL East

When Brian McCann began the 2005 season with the Double-A Mississippi Braves, he had to wonder about his future in the Atlanta organization. The big club's everyday backstop, Johnny Estrada, wasn't going anywhere: he hit .314 the previous season and won a Silver Slugger Award. McCann also had to look over his shoulder at Class-A catcher Jarrod Saltalamacchia, who was a year younger and perhaps the best prospect in the entire Braves system. Then fate intervened to launch McCann's major-league career. Estrada's backup went down with an injury in June 2005 and the Braves needed to call up one of their youngsters. Saltalamacchia wasn't ready yet, so the job fell to McCann. By the end of 2006, he was not only the Braves' number-one man behind the dish, he was arguably the best-hitting catcher in the National League.

McCann had the advantage of being a hometown favorite. Like his close friend and teammate, Jeff Francoeur, the six-foot-three catcher grew up in the Atlanta area. He was seven years old in 1991, when Bobby Cox took over as the Braves' manager and led the team to their first of 14 consecutive postseason appearances, a streak that was still alive when McCann joined the club in 2005. The 21-year-old made his big-league debut on June 10, singled in his first at-bat, and then knocked his first home run the next day. He batted .278 in that abbreviated first season — including a .347 clip with runners on base — and did an outstanding job of handling the Braves' pitching staff. John Smoltz was so impressed that he asked to have McCann as his battery mate every time he went to the mound. The honeymoon continued into the postseason, as McCann caught Smoltz's Game 2 start against the Astros in the NLDS. In the second inning of that match, he ripped a 2–0 pitch from Roger Clemens over the center-field wall for a three-run homer to lead his club to a 7–1 romp.

Unfortunately for McCann, that would be the only game Atlanta won in the 2005 playoffs.

During the offseason the Braves traded Estrada to Arizona and installed McCann in a full-time role for 2006. He responded with a torrid couple of months, and on May 20 he was leading the NL with a .350 average. That night, however, he took a throw from right field as the Diamondbacks' Eric Byrnes tried to score from first on a double. Byrnes collided with McCann and the catcher had to leave the game with a bad ankle sprain. He wound up missing two weeks, though he returned in mid-June and stayed hot enough to earn a spot as the National League's reserve catcher at the All-Star Game. Later in July, he stroked home runs in five consecutive games as he continued to pile up the RBIs. On the season, McCann drove in 93 runs and batted .471 with two outs and runners in scoring position. His ankle injury caused him to fall 10 plate appearances shy of qualifying for the batting title, but even if he had gone hitless in those additional at-bats he still would have finished sixth, a remarkable achievement for a 22-year-old catcher. His .333 average, 24 home runs and .961 OPS were enough to make him the league's Silver Slugger at the position. The taint on McCann's breakout season, however, was that the Braves' run of consecutive division titles came to an end.

McCann signed a six-year contract extension in spring training 2007 that may keep him in Atlanta until 2013. (A few months later, the Braves traded Saltalamacchia to Texas to acquire Mark Teixeira and Ron Mahay.) After batting .345 in the first three weeks of April, McCann was struck on the ring finger of his left hand while attempting to lay down a sacrifice bunt. A couple of weeks later he aggravated the injury when an opponent's swing hit him in the glove. By May 19 his average had dropped almost 70 points and it hovered around .270 the rest of the way, though he still finished with 38 doubles, 18 home runs and 92 RBIs in 132 games.

Looking ahead, the analysts at *Baseball Prospectus* expect Brian McCann to be a .300 hitter for at least the next four seasons. Joe Mauer of the Twins is the only other young catcher that promises as much, and McCann has considerably more pop in his bat, with several 25-homer campaigns likely in his future. If he lives up to those expectations, he'll be a major factor in helping the Braves revive their tradition of October glory.

$ 24.95

GATE 16

SECTION UPPER

SEAT A17

R5DR752

7JUNE08

CAREER HIGHLIGHTS

- only player in Braves history to homer in first postseason at-bat (2005)
- only MLB catcher to post a .300 average and 20 home runs in 2006
- selected to the NL All-Star Team in 2006 and 2007

29 CATCHER

Brian MⁱCANN

jorge
POSADA

During spring training of 2007, Jorge Posada approached the Yankees about a contract extension. His deal was set to expire at the end of that season, and he wanted to re-sign with New York rather than becoming a free agent. The Yankees' brass rebuffed him, however, probably figuring that the 35-year-old Puerto Rican's value would decline after some 1,300 games behind the plate. That was a decision they wound up regretting, as Posada had a career year and pushed his stock higher than ever.

The Yankees drafted Posada as a shortstop and second baseman, but even in Class-A, it was apparent that he lacked the speed to be a middle infielder at the major-league level — particularly with the Yankees, who were also grooming a kid named Derek Jeter. So before the 1992 season, the organization trained him to be a catcher, a challenge that Posada embraced until he suffered a broken leg and badly dislocated ankle in a home-plate collision in Triple-A in 1994. He was a little gun shy after that season-ending injury, but was back behind the plate the following year and earned a call-up just in time to get a taste of the postseason in 1995.

In 1997 Posada played his first full campaign as a backup for everyday catcher Joe Girardi, who would become the Yankees' manager 11 years later. By the following season, Posada was hitting well enough (17 home runs in 111 games) to wrest the starting job away from Girardi. He was also earning accolades for the way

CAREER HIGHLIGHTS

- has more home runs (177) and RBIs (693) than any other major-league catcher from 2000–07

- posted a .969 OPS in 2007, the highest ever by an AL catcher over 35

- named to five All-Star Teams (2000–03, 2007)

20 CATCHER

Jorge POSADA

he handled the hurlers, and on May 17 he caught David Wells' perfect game. The powerhouse Yankees cruised through the playoffs in 1998, and Posada was 3-for-9 with a home run in his first Fall Classic, a four-game sweep over the San Diego Padres.

Posada caught 142 games in 2000 and came into his own as a hitter: he batted .287 with 28 home runs, 35 doubles and a .417 OBP, courtesy of 107 walks, still a career-high. Making his third straight World Series appearance that October, Posada was Roger Clemens' battery mate in Game 2, when the Rocket famously threw a broken bat in the direction of the Mets' Mike Piazza. It fell to the catcher to settle his pitcher down, and he did just that, helping Clemens through eight innings of two-hit, shutout ball. The Yankees held off a ninth-inning charge to win that game and eventually took the series in five.

Between 2000 and 2003, Posada won four straight Silver Sluggers and was named to the All-Star Team each season. He emerged during this stretch as the American League's best-hitting catcher: he batted a combined .278, averaged 25 homers, and in 2002 rapped 40 doubles to establish a club mark for receivers. The following season he drove in 101 runs, and his 30 long balls matched Yogi Berra's best season to give him a share of that franchise record as well. His outstanding performance earned him five first-place votes in the 2003 MVP balloting.

One of the most durable catchers around, Posada had backstopped more than 130 games for seven straight seasons by the time the last year of his contract rolled around.

At this point in a catcher's career, the daily abuse tends to take its toll on the back and legs, usually leading to a drop in offense. That's why Posada's 2007 season was such a surprise. The Yankee veteran hit .325 with 25 doubles before the break to earn his first All-Star selection in four years. Remarkably, his second half was even better: he swatted the ball at a .355 clip (including .395 in September) as the Yankees rallied from their slow start to win the wild card spot. He finished the year at .338, fourth in the league and 41 points higher than his previous best. His 42 doubles and 20 homers also helped Posada to a career-high .543 slugging percentage and his fifth Silver Slugger.

One knock against Posada is that his postseason performance has been unimpressive. He's certainly not lacking experience — he's played in a staggering 96 playoff games — yet his lifetime average is .236, including .208 in five World Series appearances. His October woes continued in his otherwise stellar 2007 campaign when he went 2-for-15 in the ALDS against Cleveland, including a strikeout to end the deciding fourth game. Nevertheless, Posada had some impressive numbers to bring to the bargaining table a few weeks later, and he wound up signing a four-year deal with the Yankees worth over $52 million — far more than he would have commanded seven months earlier.

ivan
RODRIGUEZ

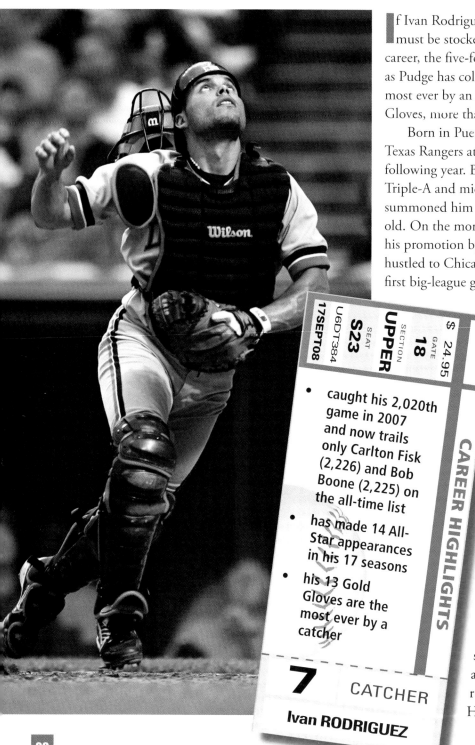

If Ivan Rodriguez has a trophy case in his home, it must be stocked like Fort Knox. During his 17-year career, the five-foot-nine, 190-pound sparkplug known as Pudge has collected seven Silver Slugger Awards, the most ever by an AL catcher, and a staggering 13 Gold Gloves, more than any backstop in history.

Born in Puerto Rico, Rodriguez signed with the Texas Rangers at age 16 and made his pro debut the following year. By 1991 he had worked his way up to Triple-A and midway through that season the Rangers summoned him to the majors as a fresh-faced 19-year-old. On the morning of June 20, Rodriguez celebrated his promotion by marrying his girlfriend, and then hustled to Chicago's brand new ballpark to play his first big-league game. The opposing catcher that night was the original Pudge: 43-year-old Carlton Fisk of the White Sox, who was playing his last full season. No one knew it at the time, but the game was an historic meeting between two future Hall of Famers at opposite ends of their careers. Both Fisk and Rodriguez threw out two attempted base stealers that night, and the teenaged Pudge collected his first hit: a two-run single that helped the Rangers come back to win in the ninth inning.

In his sophomore season, Rodriguez was selected to the All-Star Team, the first of what would become a string of 10 consecutive trips to the Midsummer Classic. Prospective thieves soon learned that his arm was a cannon: at his peak he would nail half of the runners who attempted to steal on him. His hitting developed quickly as well: by

---

$ 24.95
GATE 18
SECTION UPPER
SEAT S23
U6DT384
17SEPT08

CAREER HIGHLIGHTS

- caught his 2,020th game in 2007 and now trails only Carlton Fisk (2,226) and Bob Boone (2,225) on the all-time list

- has made 14 All-Star appearances in his 17 seasons

- his 13 Gold Gloves are the most ever by a catcher

7 CATCHER

Ivan RODRIGUEZ

1995, he'd pushed his batting average to .303, the first of eight straight seasons of .300 or better, a feat no AL catcher has ever matched. Two years later, he had his first 20-homer season and was looking like an MVP in the making. He fulfilled that promise in 1999 with one of the best all-around seasons ever recorded by a catcher: he batted .332, set a league record for home runs by a catcher (35) and became the first AL backstop ever to collect 30 homers, 100 runs and 100 RBIs. He even stole 25 bases to become the only catcher in the 20–20 club. His MVP that year capped a run of six consecutive seasons in which he won both the Gold Glove and the Silver Slugger. It was also the third season in which the Rangers won the AL West only to fall to the Yankees in the first round of the postseason.

Before the 2003 campaign began, Pudge signed with the Florida Marlins and played his one and only season in the National League. The Marlins knew that their talented but green pitching staff would benefit from the experience of a veteran like Rodriguez. His hot bat helped the Fish go 17–7 in July, and the second-half surge propelled them past the Phillies in the wild card race. In his fourth playoff appearance, Pudge was at his best, batting .353 in the NLDS before popping two homers and driving in 10 runs against the Cubs to take

MVP honors in the Championship Series. He capped it off by catching Josh Beckett's brilliant shutout in Game 6 as the Marlins took out the Yankees to win the World Series.

Rodriguez was back in the AL the following season after signing a four-year deal with the Detroit Tigers. Picking up right where he'd left off, he grabbed his seventh Silver Slugger by batting .334 with 19 home runs, and he collected the 2,000th hit and 1,000th RBI of his career during his first year in Detroit. With Pudge's help — he has been an All-Star in each of his four seasons since returning to the junior loop — the Tigers went from perennial losers to a World Series appearance in 2006.

While Rodriguez continues to be one of the best defensive catchers in the game, he has shown a surprising lack of patience at the plate in recent years. He walked just 11 times in 2005, and in 2007 he drew a mere nine free passes in 515 plate appearances — far and away the worst mark in the majors, and a big reason why his OBP was a dreary .297. Despite that worrying trend, the Tigers picked up his option for 2008. If he stays healthy and productive over the next two seasons, he's set to become the all-time leader in games played by a catcher.

BATMEN

travis HAFNER

Travis Hafner may be the Rodney Dangerfield of baseball. The Cleveland Indians' rugged, bald-headed designated hitter has been one of the most feared batsmen in the game for the past four seasons — particularly in 2006, when he hit .308 with 42 home runs despite missing a month. "Per plate appearance," said *Baseball Prospectus 2007*, "Hafner was the best hitter in the American League." ESPN's Jayson Stark called him the most underappreciated DH, while baseball-reference.com describes him as "quite possibly the most underrated player in major league baseball." Hafner has finished in the top eight in MVP voting twice, and in 2006 he led the league in slugging (.659) and OPS (1.098). So, how many times has he been selected to play in the All-Star Game? Zero. In 2006 he even hit a record five grand slams before the break and was still passed over in favor of David Ortiz and Jim Thome.

The big guy everyone calls Pronk never got much respect as a prospect either. He went to a tiny North Dakota high school where he had just seven classmates — not even enough to field a baseball team. He attracted few scouts in college and was chosen in the 31st round of the 1996 draft by the Texas Rangers. He didn't have a decent year in the minors until 1999, and was finally called up in 2002. The Rangers had no room on the roster for a big, slow power hitter who could barely play first base, so they dealt him to Cleveland for two no-names. By 2004 the Rangers were wishing they could have that deal back, as Hafner batted .311 with 28 homers and 109 RBIs.

Part of the reason for Hafner's low profile is that fans don't see him very often. While many designated hitters are former position players who are now long in the tooth, Hafner has always been primarily a DH. He has never been fast, and he is hampered by a chronic elbow problem that makes throwing difficult. If that weren't enough, pitchers seem to derive great enjoyment from bouncing baseballs off of Pronk's six-foot-three frame. He missed two months in 2003 after his big toe was broken by a pitch. The following year Hafner escaped injury despite a league-leading 17 HBPs, but he wasn't so lucky in 2005: he was put on the disabled list with post-concussive symptoms after Chisox ace Mark Buehrle beaned him in the face. Most painful of all, however, was the pitch that broke his hand on September 1, 2006. He was on pace for 51 homers and 143 RBIs before missing the final 29 games of the season. That pitch may have cost Hafner the MVP award.

Hafner has a good eye and hits for average as well as power, but he isn't one to use the whole field. He's a dead pull hitter from the left side of the plate, and teams often use the shift on him, positioning three infielders between first and second. Pronk is a streaky player who can carry his club when he gets hot. At the start of 2005, he did not tally his first home run until his 95th at-bat, the longest homerless streak of his career, but later went yard in six straight games in September. He had seven homers after just 11 games of the 2006 season — the fastest start in the club's 106-year history — and then hit 13 more in August before breaking his hand.

His production dropped significantly in 2007, and some speculated that he was distracted in the first half by contract negotiations. After the All-Star break, the Indians signed their DH through 2012. Even with the vote of confidence, Hafner turned in a disappointing season, as his average dropped more than 40 points and he hit a mere 24 home runs, though he did manage to reach 100 RBIs for the fourth straight season and drew a career-high 102 walks. When the Indians cruised into the postseason and eliminated the Yankees, one of the biggest blows of the series was Hafner's walk-off single in the 11th inning of Game 2. He went on to hit .148 in the Championship Series, but Indians fans weren't throwing brickbats after his off year. In Cleveland, at least, Pronk gets the respect he deserves.

$ 24.95
GATE 18
SECTION CLUB
SEAT CC8
H2BV/256
28MAY08

CAREER HIGHLIGHTS

- second Indians player ever to record 40 homers, 100 walks, 100 runs and 100 RBIs in the same season (2006)

- tied MLB record for grand slams in one season with six (2006)

- compiled an on-base percentage over .400 from 2004–06

48 DESIGNATED HITTER

Travis HAFNER

david
ORTIZ

When the game is on the line in the ninth inning or beyond, the man you want at the plate is David Ortiz. During his career, Big Papi has ended 16 regular-season games with walk-off hits. But it's not the regular-season ones that made him a hero in Red Sox Nation. It was the unprecedented three game-winners he collected in the 2004 postseason, as Boston finally won its first World Series since 1918.

Ortiz's emergence as one of the most deadly hitters in the American League was entirely unexpected. Drafted by the Seattle Mariners in 1992, he was dealt to the Minnesota Twins four years later as an afterthought in a deal to acquire journeyman Dave Hollins. He debuted with the Twins in 1997 and played 86 games the following year, but the team demoted him to Triple-A in 1999. For the next three unremarkable seasons, Ortiz played sporadically because of injuries, and the Twins saw no place for him in their future. In December 2002 they tried to trade him, and when no one showed interest, they released him.

The Red Sox decided to take a chance on the 27-year-old, who had a below-average glove and whose most productive season was 20 homers and 75 RBIs. By the middle of May 2003 the cast-off was batting .205 with a single home run for a dysfunctional team, and he was asking to be traded. Instead, the Bosox dumped the troublesome Shea Hillenbrand to make room for Ortiz in the everyday lineup. Big Papi embraced his new role as full-time DH and from July onward he slugged 28 home runs, helping Boston turn things around and win the wild card race. But the Curse of the Bambino struck again in the form of Yankee third baseman Aaron Boone, whose 11th-inning homer in Game 7 of the ALCS ended the Red Sox' season.

Hitting third in front of Manny Ramirez in 2004, Ortiz was part of a devastating one-two punch. He led the AL with 91 extra-base hits (including 41 homers) and he drove in 139 runs. Once again securing the wild card spot, the Red Sox faced the Anaheim Angels in the American League Division Series. They won the first two games and completed the sweep when Ortiz homered in the 10th inning to end Game 3.

That set up a rematch with the Yankees, and it was one of the greatest playoff series in history. The Red Sox dropped the first two games in New York, then returned to Fenway, only to be humiliated by a score of 19–8 in Game 3. Trailing 4–3 in the bottom of the ninth in Game 4, with the untouchable Mariano Rivera on the mound, it looked to be all over. But the Red Sox tied it to force extra innings, and Ortiz blasted a home run in the 12th to stave off elimination. In the next match, Ortiz homered in the eighth to help the Sox erase a 4–2 Yankees lead and force extra innings again. In the bottom of the 14th, with two outs and two men on,

Ortiz lined a single to center field for his second straight walk-off hit and his third of the playoffs. Boston completed the most improbable comeback in baseball history by winning the next two games to oust the Yankees (Ortiz was an easy choice for series MVP). The Red Sox then went on to sweep the St. Louis Cardinals, claiming their first championship in 86 years.

Amazingly, Ortiz actually improved his numbers in 2005, upping his home run total to 47 and collecting a league-leading 148 RBIs. He followed that up with an AL-best 54 homers in 2006, setting a Red Sox record and a new mark for designated hitters. He added to his reputation as a peerless clutch hitter with five walk-off hits, including three game-ending homers.

Ortiz was bothered by a sore knee in 2007 and he admitted it would likely require offseason surgery. You wouldn't have known it from his performance, however. While his home run total slipped to 35, he batted .332 with 52 doubles (both career highs) and was red-hot when it mattered: he compiled a 1.341 OPS in September as the Red Sox locked up first place in AL East. Big Papi didn't have any of his signature walk-off moments in the postseason, but he batted .370 with six doubles, three homers, 10 RBIs an OBP of .525 as Boston won its second World Series in four years.

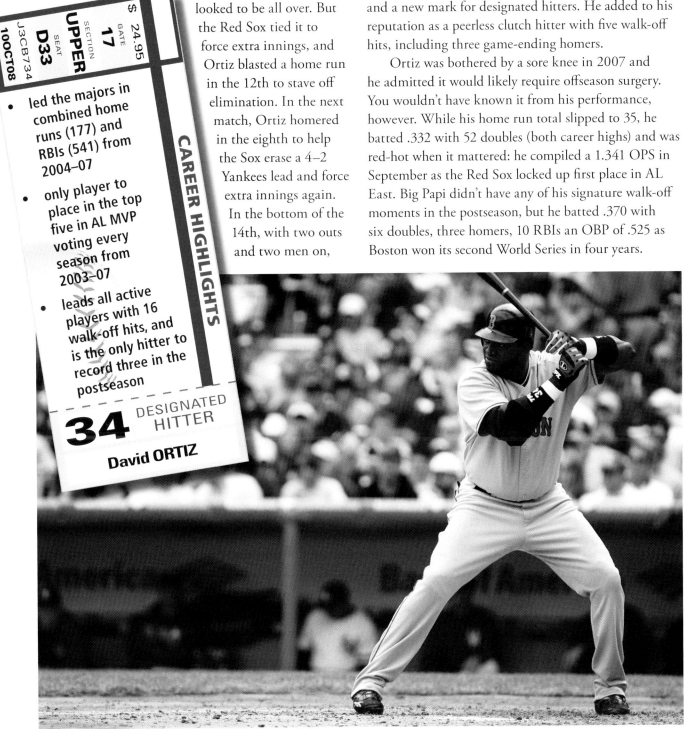

$ 24.95
GATE 17
SECTION UPPER
SEAT D33
J3CB734
10OCT08

CAREER HIGHLIGHTS

- led the majors in combined home runs (177) and RBIs (541) from 2004–07

- only player to place in the top five in AL MVP voting every season from 2003–07

- leads all active players with 16 walk-off hits, and is the only hitter to record three in the postseason

34 DESIGNATED HITTER

David ORTIZ

gary SHEFFIELD

When the Detroit Tigers signed Gary Sheffield before the 2007 season, they could have made a few predictions based on his past performance. He'd probably spend part of the year on the disabled list (10 previous stints), be suspended for his on-field antics (five prior offenses), and at some point would likely accuse his coaches, teammates or the front office of being racists. Finally, he might be expected to perform brilliantly at the plate: he had, after all, recorded 30-homer, 100-RBI years for all but one of his six previous employers. You can say a lot about Gary Sheffield's personality flaws, but no one can accuse of him of being unable to hit.

Role models were hard to come by in the tough Tampa neighborhood where Sheffield grew up. But Gary played a lot of baseball with the one mentor who was about his age: his uncle, just four years older, was future Cy Young–winner Dwight Gooden, and back then he was already throwing a blazing fastball. That early batting practice helped the young Sheffield develop the bat speed that would later make him a superstar.

After being drafted in the first round by the Milwaukee Brewers in 1986, Sheffield made his big-league debut at shortstop when he was only 19. His first four years were difficult. Sheffield alienated his teammates with ill-advised comments, and when he was moved from short to third base to make room for Billy Spiers, who is white, he wrote his ticket out of Milwaukee by publicly stating that

the move was racially motivated. The Brewers traded their petulant infielder to the San Diego Padres during spring training in 1992.

Sheffield thrived in his new surroundings. Just 23 years old, he hit .330 to become the youngest batting champion in 30 years, won his first Silver Slugger Award at third base with 33 home runs and 100 RBIs, and finished third in the MVP voting. Perhaps most impressive, he struck out just 40 times. Midway through the next season, however, Sheffield was dealt to the Florida Marlins. In 1996, his first full season with the Fish — and now playing right field — he belted 42 homers and drove in 120 runs to go along with an OBP of .465. He then helped the Marlins to their improbable victory in the World Series in 1997, homering in all three playoff series.

Sheffield went on to become a terror at the plate in Los Angeles and Atlanta. He set a Dodgers record with 43 home runs in 2000, and a Braves mark for RBIs with 132 in 2003. When he became a free agent at the end of that season, Sheffield made it known that he wanted to play

in New York, and got his wish when the Yankees signed him for $13 million a year. Sheffield was outstanding during his first two years in pinstripes, averaging .290 with 35 home runs and 121 RBIs.

Then he missed most of 2006 with a wrist injury, and when the Yankees acquired Bobby Abreu to play right field that July, Sheffield became expendable. He was traded in the offseason to the Tigers, who installed him as a DH for the first time in his career.

There were few surprises in Sheff's first campaign in Detroit. He spent a couple of weeks on the DL with a shoulder injury late in the season, was suspended in June for throwing a broken bat in the direction of an umpire, and made headlines by saying that Joe Torre, his former manager in New York, treated black players with disrespect. His offensive production was well below what he accomplished in his prime, but he still posted a .378 OBP and swatted 25 home runs despite his injuries. His 38-year-old legs even stole 22 bases, his best total since 1998. Time will tell whether he'll finish his remarkable career in Detroit, or whether those legs will eventually be run out of town.

$ 24.95
GATE
24
SECTION
UPPER
HH6
SEAT
T5SF873
16OCT08

CAREER HIGHLIGHTS

- only player in history to represent five different clubs at the All-Star Game
- only player to collect 100 RBIs in a season for five teams, and one of two to hit 30 homers in a season for five clubs
- has more walks than strikeouts in 16 of his 20 seasons and a career on-base percentage of .397

3 DESIGNATED HITTER

Gary SHEFFIELD

jim THOME

It wasn't easy for Jim Thome to leave Cleveland. The big corner infielder had been drafted by the Indians way back in 1989 and established himself as one of the greatest power hitters in franchise history, with seven consecutive seasons of 30 or more homers. Thome was a key part of the Indians' resurgence as the team reached the postseason six times from 1995 to 2001 after decades of futility. On top of it all, his friendly demeanor, tireless work ethic and community involvement made Thome the most popular athlete in the city. When he became a free agent in 2002, he was even willing to accept less than his market value to stay in Cleveland. But the team would not grant his request for a six-year contract, and Thome left to join the National League. After three seasons with the Philadelphia Phillies, he was back in the American League Central, this time with the rival Chicago White Sox. If he still misses Cleveland, his numbers haven't shown it — for Thome, it seems, home is wherever he swings his bat.

Thome was born in Peoria, Illinois, into a blue-collar baseball family that taught him the value of hard work.

$ 24.95
GATE 20
SECTION FIELD
SEAT K15
H3SD469
15JUNE08

CAREER HIGHLIGHTS

- ranks 22nd all-time with 507 career home runs
- has a career OBP of .409 and ranks 19th all-time with 1,459 bases on balls
- has hit 17 postseason home runs (fifth all-time) and is the only player with two playoff grand slams (1998 and 1999)

25 DESIGNATED HITTER

Jim THOME

He bounced between the big leagues and the minors for three years until the Indians made him their everyday third baseman in the strike-shortened 1994 campaign. The following season, Thome hit .314 with 25 home runs as the Indians won 100 games and their first American League pennant since the Korean War. The turning point in their ALCS victory over Seattle was his mammoth two-run homer in the pivotal fifth game.

Thome erupted in 1996 with 38 home runs, 116 RBIs and an OBP of .450 — thanks to a .311 batting average coupled with 123 bases on balls — to earn a Silver Slugger Award. Just 25 years old, Thome was already showing the selective eye that would eventually place him third among active players in walks, behind only Barry Bonds and Frank Thomas. When he moved across the diamond to first base in 1997, he slugged 40 homers and was selected to his first All-Star Team. He missed five weeks of the 1998 season when he broke his hand in August, but returned for the stretch drive and then went deep four times in the postseason against the Yankees, setting an ALCS record.

Between 1999 and 2002, Thome terrorized pitchers with home run totals of 33, 37, 49 and 52. That final total, a franchise record, was part of a monster season where he batted .304 and led the league with a slugging percentage of .677. After the 2002 season, Thome was on his way to Philadelphia, and pitchers in the senior loop were none too pleased to see him. Surpassing all predictions, he hit 47 and 42 homers in his first two seasons with the Phillies. But he injured his lower back in May 2005, and had season-ending elbow surgery in August. In 59 games, he batted just .207 with seven home runs. His spot at first base was filled by the eventual Rookie of the Year, Ryan Howard, and there was no way Thome would be back in Philly for 2006. He was traded to the White Sox, and while he looked forward to playing in his home state, the big question was whether he would be able to regain his swing. At least his return to the AL meant that his big frame would not have to patrol the infield — instead, he would be the White Sox' designated hitter.

Once again, Thome won over his new team with an outstanding year, launching 42 homers, driving in 109 runs and winning AL Comeback Player of the Year in 2006. By reaching the 40-homer plateau again, he joined Alex Rodriguez as the only other player to reach that mark with three different clubs. The following year, despite a strained rib cage in April and back spasms in August, he belted another 35 long balls and drove in 96 runs in 130 games. The most memorable of those games came on September 16 against the Angels. With the score tied 7–7 in the bottom of the ninth, Thome turned on a full-count fastball and hit a bomb over the left-center wall for a walk-off home run. The blast was the 500th of his career, and almost certainly a ticket to Cooperstown.

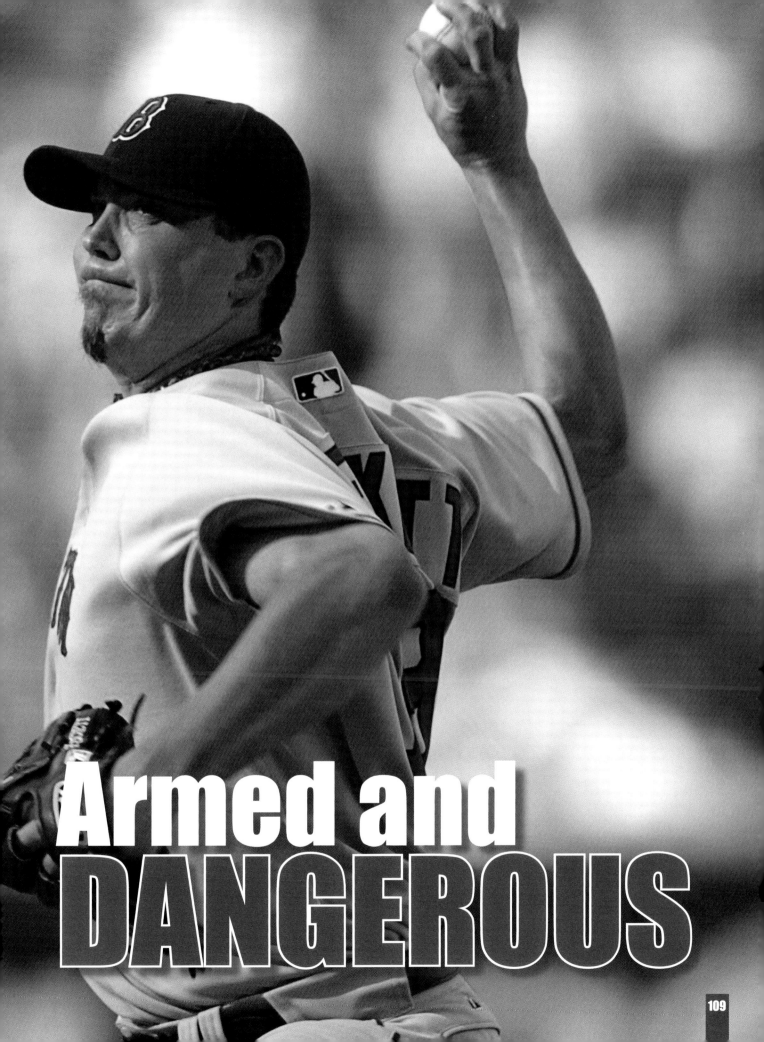

Armed and
DANGEROUS

josh BECKETT

BOSTON RED SOX ◆ AL East

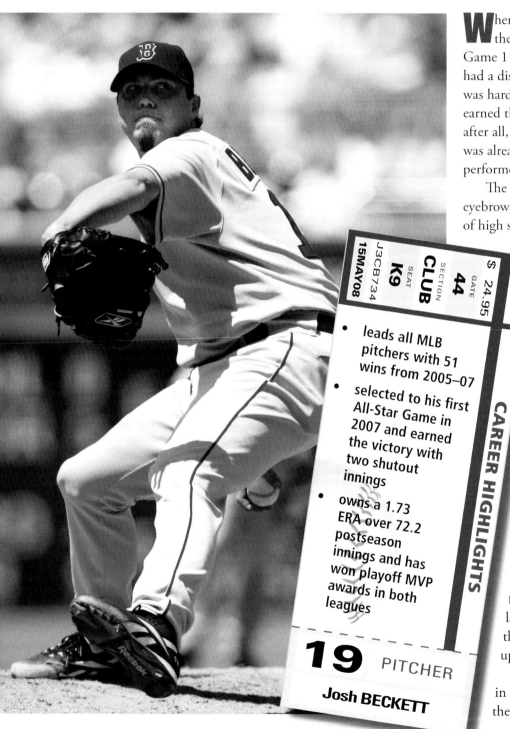

When Josh Beckett walked to the mound at Fenway Park for Game 1 of the 2007 World Series, he had a distinctly arrogant swagger. Yet it was hard to argue that Beckett hadn't earned the right to strut — this was, after all, a pitcher who at 27 years old was already one of the best postseason performers ever.

The Florida Marlins raised some eyebrows when they drafted Beckett out of high school with their second-overall pick in 1999. It is extremely unusual to use such an early draft choice on a high school pitcher, but the club felt he could be the center of their rebuilding effort — and he was. Beckett made his first big-league appearance two years later, hurling six magnificent innings in which he gave up one hit, and his fine September helped him secure a spot in the Marlins' young rotation for the following year. The 22-year-old pitched well in 2002, but he developed a frustrating problem with a blister on his right middle finger. The recurring ailment landed him on the DL three times that season, and continues to crop up occasionally.

Beckett missed over a month in 2003 with an elbow injury, and the Marlins struggled mightily in

$ 24.95

GATE 44

SECTION CLUB

SEAT K9

J3CB734

15MAY08

CAREER HIGHLIGHTS

- leads all MLB pitchers with 51 wins from 2005–07
- selected to his first All-Star Game in 2007 and earned the victory with two shutout innings
- owns a 1.73 ERA over 72.2 postseason innings and has won playoff MVP awards in both leagues

19 PITCHER

Josh BECKETT

his absence. On June 18 they were 34–39 and in last place, 14 games back. Aided by his return, the Marlins went on an amazing late-season run that saw them capture the wild card spot. At this point in his career, Beckett was little more than a cocky young fireballer who had shown a few flashes of greatness, but the 2003 postseason would showcase what he was really made of. In Game 1 of the Division Series, his October debut, he allowed two hits and one run over seven innings, though he took the loss as the Giants' Jason Schmidt tossed a shutout. The Cubs roughed him up in Game 1 of the NLCS (the Fish went on to win anyway), but he returned to hurl a gem in Game 5: he went the distance, surrendering only two hits and striking out 11. When starter Mark Redman got into trouble in Game 7, Beckett worked four innings of stellar relief, giving the Marlins a chance to come back from a 6–5 deficit and advance to the World Series.

Beckett was simply masterful in his first Fall Classic. In Game 3 he struck out 10 Yankees and held their sluggers to two runs before exiting in the eighth. Unfortunately for him, the Marlins scored only once, and the bullpen allowed four more tallies in the ninth to end any hope of a comeback. That put the Yanks up 2–1 in the series, but the Marlins stormed back by winning the next two. Beckett took the ball for Game 6 at Yankee Stadium on three days' rest and proceeded to mow down the Bronx Bombers. When it was over, he had allowed a paltry five hits in a 2–0 complete-game

victory to give the Marlins their second championship. Beckett's 1.10 ERA made him the World Series MVP, and his 47 postseason strikeouts tied the MLB record.

After two more fine seasons in Florida, Beckett was dealt along with Mike Lowell to Boston in a deal that sent Hanley Ramirez and Anibal Sanchez to the Marlins. He won over Red Sox Nation by winning his first three starts in 2006 and eventually pushed his record to 10–3, but then fell to 6–8 the rest of the way, finishing with the worst ERA of his career (5.01). He seemed to have everything worked out by 2007, however. Beckett won his first nine decisions, and on September 21 he became the only 20-game winner in the majors. He also set career marks in WHIP (1.14) and strikeouts (194), while walking just 40 batters in 200 innings.

Beckett's performance in the 2007 postseason was about as good as they get. He opened the Division Series with a four-hit shutout against the Angels, and then beat C.C. Sabathia and the Indians in Game 1 and Game 5 of the ALCS to earn series MVP honors. The Colorado Rockies got to him for a run in the second inning of the World Series lid-lifter, but Beckett shut them down over the next five, striking out nine en route to a 13–1 drubbing. In four playoff starts, Beckett was 4–0 with a 1.20 ERA and struck out 35 batters while walking just two. With October numbers like that, Beckett might someday find himself with another blister on his finger — this one from all the rings.

mark
BUEHRLE

As pitching prospects go, Mark Buehrle was about as unpromising as they come. He did not even make his high school baseball team until his junior year, and when no major universities came knocking, Buehrle ended up at Jefferson College in his home state of Missouri. A perfect 8–0 record in his freshman season finally caught the scouts' eyes. The Chicago White Sox decided to spend a lowly 38th round draft pick on him in 1998 and clearly were not expecting much.

But the young lefty turned out to be a quick study. Buehrle had an average fastball, but also possessed a good slider, a curve and a changeup, and could throw all of them for strikes: in 218 minor-league innings he walked just 33 batters. In July 2000 the White Sox — who by then had built a 9½-game lead atop the AL Central — were convinced he was for real, and they called him up. A major-league pennant race was a high-pressure situation for a pitcher who 12 months earlier had been throwing to Class-A batters. But Buehrle displayed the poise he would soon be renowned for, and in 25 relief appearances and three starts he went 4–1. Opponents soon learned one of his other trademarks: his deadly pickoff move, almost indistinguishable from his motion toward home plate, which he used to erase any runner who leaned too far toward second.

In spring training the following year, Buehrle earned a spot in the starting rotation. After struggling early, he put together a string of 24 scoreless innings and won five straight to turn his season around. He finished at 16–8 with a 3.29 ERA and led the league with a stingy 1.07 WHIP. In 2002 he won 19 games for a mediocre White Sox club and made his first All-Star Team as he emerged as one of the finest left-handers in the American League. While he rarely overpowers hitters, Buehrle uses his excellent command to get ahead in the count and induce ground-ball outs.

When Ozzie Guillen took over as manager in 2004, Buehrle became the workhorse of the staff, leading the

AL in innings pitched (he would do so again in 2005) — and winning 16 games. The Chisox finished second that year, but in the middle of the campaign they picked up starters Freddy Garcia and Jose Contreras, and then added Orlando Hernandez in the offseason. In 2005 — with Buehrle as the ace and Jon Garland posting a surprising 18 wins — the White Sox had the best rotation in the league. Buehrle charged out of the gate, winning 10 of his first 11 decisions, and earned the honor of starting the All-Star Game. He tossed two innings and struck out three to earn the victory without allowing a run. He cooled off in the second half, but finished the year at 16–8 with a 3.19 ERA, third-best in the league. More importantly, the White Sox won 99 games and the AL Central title. Buehrle earned the victory in Game 2 of the ALDS against the wild-card winning Red Sox, and then tossed a complete-game gem against the Angels in the second match of the ALCS, helping Chicago to its first pennant since 1959.

In the 2005 Fall Classic, Buehrle started Game 2 against the Houston Astros and did not

$ 24.95
GATE **19**
SECTION **FIELD**
SEAT **AA2**
B3KJ356
22JUNE08

- only White Sox pitcher ever to start at least 30 games in seven consecutive seasons (2001–07)
- leads all AL hurlers in innings pitched (1,578) since 2001
- has allowed 32 stolen bases in more than 1,600 innings pitched, while his catchers have thrown out 45 runners

CAREER HIGHLIGHTS

56 PITCHER

Mark BUEHRLE

figure in the decision, but he made his contribution — and World Series history — two nights later.

Game 3 was a marathon that stretched into the 14th inning before the White Sox finally scored two in the top of the frame. When Houston put two men on in the bottom of the inning, the pivotal match was suddenly in jeopardy. Having already used eight pitchers, the depleted Sox turned to Buehrle, who got Adam Everett to pop up for the final out. It was the first time a pitcher in a World Series had earned a save after starting the previous game, and it stuck a fork in the Astros, who were swept the next day.

The White Sox had a dismal 2007, but Buehrle's third start of the season was one of the few highlights. On April 18 against the Texas Rangers, he took a perfect game into the fifth inning before walking Sammy Sosa with one out. He promptly picked off Sosa and then retired the next 13 batters for a no-hit masterpiece. Three months later, Buehrle signed a contract extension that will keep him in Chicago until at least 2011.

roy HALLADAY

Since 2002 the Toronto Blue Jays have had an inconsistent rotation: other than Ted Lilly in 2006, the starting staff has not had a 15-win season by anyone whose name isn't Roy Halladay. The six-foot-six righty, meanwhile, has won more games than any other starter in the American League.

Known to teammates and fans as Doc, Halladay has become Toronto's best remedy against prolonged slumps. From 2005 through 2007, Halladay's record following a Blue Jays loss is 24–8, while the team is 31–12 when he goes to the mound after a defeat. And in an era that has become obsessive about pitch counts, Halladay's outstanding control and fast pace on the mound allow him to work deep into his starts and give the bullpen a rest. In 2007 he tossed seven complete games — only two *teams* in the majors had more. No club can ask any more of its ace.

Roy Halladay grew up in a suburb of Denver, and after an outstanding career at Arvada West High School he was the Blue Jays' first-round pick in 1995. The organization fast-tracked him to Triple-A, where he won nine games in 1998. That earned him a September call-up, and in his second major-league start the 21-year-old tossed an absolute gem against the Detroit Tigers. By the ninth inning, he had not surrendered a hit or a walk, with the only base runner reaching on an error.

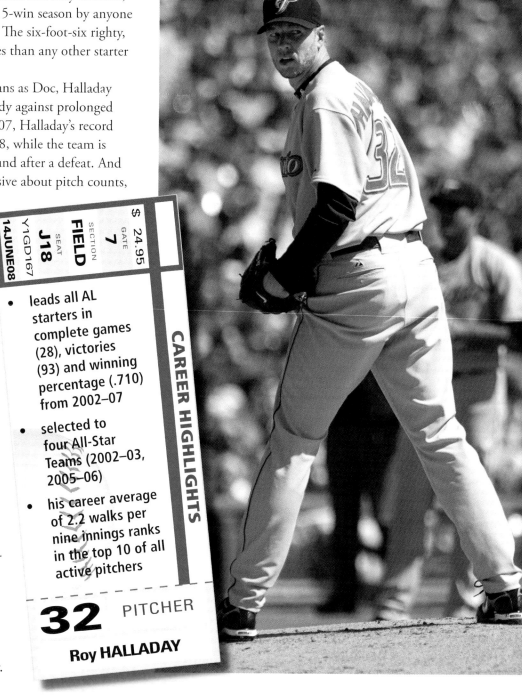

$ 24.95
GATE 7
SECTION FIELD
SEAT J18
Y1GD167
14JUNE08

CAREER HIGHLIGHTS

- leads all AL starters in complete games (28), victories (93) and winning percentage (.710) from 2002–07
- selected to four All-Star Teams (2002–03, 2005–06)
- his career average of 2.2 walks per nine innings ranks in the top 10 of all active pitchers

32 PITCHER

Roy HALLADAY

He quickly retired the first two batters in the final frame before having his no-hit bid spoiled by a pinch home run.

Following that near-perfect debut, Halladay started 18 games and worked out of the bullpen the following season, posting a 3.92 ERA, and the Blue Jays looked strong going into 2000 with a young rotation that included Chris Carpenter and Kelvim Escobar. Then Halladay imploded. After winning his first start, he was pounded in the next six, and by late July his ERA was a bloated 11.05, and he eventually found himself all the way back in Class-A.

Halladay's delivery was messed up, and so was his psychological approach. He had to learn to pitch all over again. A fastball/curveball pitcher to that point, he came to realize that he didn't have to blow every hitter away. He needed to channel his intensity, not let it throw him off his game. Doc focused on good mechanics and keeping the ball down to induce grounders. He also developed a cut fastball that would become his deadliest weapon. Halladay was transformed, and with his game together physically and mentally in 2002, he posted a 19–7 record and a 2.93 ERA, fifth best in the AL.

Halladay's 2003 season was among the best ever posted by a Toronto starter. After a rough April, Doc earned the victory in his next eleven starts and went 15–0 from May through July. In September, he tossed the majors' first 10-inning shutout in 13 years, blanking the Tigers 1–0 during a streak of 23 consecutive scoreless frames. He ended up with a league-leading 22 wins against seven losses, a 3.25 ERA, and an incredible strikeout-to-walk ratio of 6.38 (204 K's and 32 bases on balls). He was an easy choice for the American League Cy Young Award.

Two stints on the DL with shoulder problems erased any hopes of repeating that performance the following year, but the start of 2005 saw Halladay return to dominance. Before the break he was 12–4 with a sensational 0.96 WHIP and he was set to start the All-Star Game when he suffered a freak injury. On July 8, his last start before the Midsummer Classic, the Rangers' Kevin Mench smacked a line drive off Halladay's left shin, fracturing the tibia and costing him the rest of the season.

Halladay won 16 games in both 2006 and 2007, hurling more than 220 innings each year. He has continued to adjust his repertoire, adding a changeup and relying far less on strikeouts and more on ground balls — a strategy that works well on a slick-fielding team like Toronto. By throwing more sinkers and fewer cut fastballs, Halladay has also been able to avoid the arm fatigue that used to hamper him late in the season.

With veteran A.J. Burnett and young guns Dustin McGowan and Shaun Marcum following Doc to the mound in 2008, the Blue Jays may have the best starting rotation in baseball. Halladay now finds himself in the unfamiliar situation of being on a team loaded with good arms. But for now at least, he remains the staff ace.

scott KAZMIR

When Scott Kazmir pitched at Cypress Falls High School in Houston, he tossed six no-hitters, including four in a row during his junior year. Not surprisingly, when the 2002 draft approached he was the top-ranked high schooler in the country. But Kazmir had made it clear that he carried a hefty price tag, and that scared off a number of teams who might have drafted him higher. As it turned out, the deep-pocketed Mets took the young lefty with their 15th pick and paid him $2.15 million to sign.

Though barely six feet tall, Kazmir could overpower hitters with his heater, and he was dominating in the minors. By 2004, still just 20 years old, he was promoted to Double-A, where he logged a 1.73 ERA and a 0.96 WHIP in his first four starts. Meanwhile, the Mets were a game out of first in the NL East in mid-July and in need of a starter who could help them right away. Their decision was to deal Kazmir to Tampa Bay for Victor Zambrano. The swap would have been bad enough had the Mets merely mortgaged their future for short-term success. But Zambrano started just three games that year and New York finished 25 games off the mark.

Kazmir was less than excited about joining the AL's perennial whipping boy, but he recognized the chance to be a big fish in a small pond. Indeed, the Devil Rays decided their new acquisition would be best served by an almost immediate promotion to the majors. He debuted in Seattle on August 23, 2004, and hurled five shutout innings to notch his first win, becoming the youngest pitcher to win his first major-league start in almost 30 years. He won his second three weeks later by tossing six scoreless frames at Fenway to beat Pedro Martinez and the Red Sox. He was bombed in four other starts that first season, but no one was expecting consistency at this stage of Kazmir's promising career.

The Devil Rays were the only team in baseball whose ace was a 21-year-old rookie in 2005. While the rest of the rotation struggled to keep their ERAs under 6.00, Kazmir's came in at 3.77 and he set a franchise record with 174 strikeouts. The lefty gave his team many opportunities to win: he surrendered one earned run or less in 14 starts, a feat matched in the AL only by Johan Santana and Mark Buehrle. But the batters and the bullpen gave him little support and he finished the year at 10–9. He was at his best in the second half, going 7–2 with a 2.79 ERA after the break. The only knock against him was his wildness, which led to an AL-high 100 walks.

When Kazmir took the ball on April 3, 2006, he became the youngest Opening Day starter since Dwight Gooden two decades earlier. In sharp contrast with the previous year, he had an outstanding first half, defeating some of the game's top hurlers, including Roy Halladay, Curt Schilling and Dontrelle Willis. The high point came on July 3, when Kazmir tossed a two-hit shutout to beat fellow Texan Josh Beckett and the Red Sox. A week later, he was on the mound in Pittsburgh for the All-Star Game, making short work of Freddy Sanchez, Carlos Beltran and Albert Pujols. Then soreness in his shoulder landed him on the DL in late July, and when it didn't improve, the D-Rays wisely decided to rest their golden arm for the rest of the season.

Kazmir made a league-high 34 starts in 2007, going 13–9 on the strength of another second-half surge. He continues to have success with a lively fastball, a good slider and a curve, and he is working to improve his changeup to keep hitters off balance. He averaged 10.41 strikeouts per nine innings in 2007, but continued to struggle with his control. Kazmir's challenge will be to keep his pitch count down so he can work deeper into games — he has averaged less than six innings per start over his career.

With only three-plus years of service, Kazmir will not be eligible for free agency until 2010. Whether he remains with the Rays until that time depends in part on how serious Tampa Bay is about winning — and with a roster of good young hitters led by Carl Crawford and B.J. Upton, the Rays appear to be a team on the rise.

$ 24.95
GATE 5
SECTION UPPER
SEAT A19
C3ER256
11 JULY 08

CAREER HIGHLIGHTS

- led the American League with 239 strikeouts in 2007

- his 10.14 strikeouts per nine innings in 2006 was the third-best all-time for a pitcher under 23

- one of only four pitchers in the last two decades to compile three winning seasons with 10 or more victories before turning 24

19 PITCHER

Scott KAZMIR

john LACKEY

LOS ANGELES ANGELS ◆ AL West

High school football is a minor attraction in much of North America, but in John Lackey's hometown of Abilene, Texas, it's an obsession. As the quarterback on his high school squad, Lackey was playing in front of thousands of rabid fans while he was a teenager, so he knew a thing or two about the pressure of performing in big games. But even that early experience could not have fully prepared him for the assignment he received on October 27, 2002. As a rookie who had started the season in Triple-A, Lackey walked onto the field at Anaheim Stadium that evening to start Game 7 of the World Series against Barry Bonds and the San Francisco Giants.

Angels fans may have questioned the wisdom of placing a freshman pitcher in such a pressure cooker.

But Lackey had already proven his character. On September 26, his last start of the regular season, he earned the victory in a 10–5 decision over the Texas Rangers, clinching a wild card berth for his team. In the ALCS against Minnesota, Lackey threw seven shutout innings in his Game 4 start, never allowing a runner to reach second base. He also took the mound in Game 4 of the World Series — on his 24th birthday — and pitched four scoreless innings before surrendering three runs in the fifth and leaving with the game tied. (The Angels would go on to lose 4–3.) Now, here he was on the mound in the biggest game of his life. After a three-up, three-down first inning, Lackey allowed a run on a sacrifice fly in the second, and then shut down the Giants for three more innings before exiting with a 4–1

lead. Three relievers held San Francisco to two hits the rest of the way, and the Angels had their first-ever World Series championship. The cap that Lackey wore that night now rests in Cooperstown.

After that magical rookie season, Lackey's performance over the next two years was inconsistent. He was a combined 24–29 with a 4.65 ERA, though he mixed in three shutouts amid a number of rocky outings. It wasn't until 2005 that Lackey came into his own. By adding some downward movement to his fastball and improving his changeup, he allowed far fewer home runs — during one stretch he went 63 innings without serving up a gopher ball. He finished the campaign at 14–5 and cracked the league's top five in ERA with a 3.44 mark. He was third in strikeouts with 199, and his rate of 8.57 K's per nine innings was second only to Johan Santana's, though he was certainly the number-two man in the Los Angeles rotation behind Bartolo Colon, that season's Cy Young winner. Led by their two top guns, the Angels won their division and faced off against the Yankees in the ALDS. Lackey started Game 2 and had a no-decision in a 5–3 Angels win, and then returned on three days' rest to start Game 4. He allowed two hits and a lone run before leaving in the sixth, but the

Angels lost 3–2. They ousted the Yankees the next day, however, before bowing out to the White Sox in the Championship Series.

When Colon suffered a shoulder injury that kept him on the DL for most of 2006, Lackey assumed the role of the Angels' ace. During his hottest stretch that season, he strung together 30 scoreless innings, including a near-perfect game in which he gave up a leadoff double to Oakland's Mark Kotsay and then set down the next 27 consecutive batters. But while his ERA was a fine 3.56, his record was a mediocre 13–11, the result of inconsistency and a lack of run support — in five of his losses, he allowed three earned runs or fewer.

Lackey put together his best season in 2007, a year that saw him take the ball in yet more big games. In August, with Seattle close on the heels of the front-running Angels, Lackey tossed a shutout against the Mariners despite being ill. Then he beat the M's again in late September to clinch the division. His 19–9 record placed him second in the AL in wins, and his 3.01 ERA was the lowest in the loop. Lackey went into Game 1 of the ALDS on a roll, but gave up four runs in six innings, while Josh Beckett tossed a four-hit shutout for the Red Sox, who went on to sweep the series.

$ 24.95
GATE 22
SECTION UPPER
SEAT D15
J2KL123
19AUG08

CAREER HIGHLIGHTS

- first rookie starter since 1909 to win a Game 7 in the World Series (2002)
- led the American League in ERA in 2007 (3.01)
- selected to his first AL All-Star Team in 2007

41 PITCHER

John LACKEY

daisuke MATSUZAKA

$ 24.95

GATE 3

SECTION UPPER

SEAT D33

P8GC173

13JUNE08

CAREER HIGHLIGHTS

- compiled a 108–60 record and a 2.95 ERA during eight years with the Seibu Lions in Japan

- named MVP of the 2006 World Baseball Classic after going 3–0, including a win over Cuba in the championship game

- held AL batters to a .246 average during his first year in North America

18 PITCHER

Daisuke MATSUZAKA

When the Boston Red Sox signed Daisuke Matsuzaka in November 2006, the right-hander immediately became the most hyped Japanese import since Ichiro Suzuki. Promptly dubbed "Dice-K," Matsuzaka arrived in New England not only with a glowing record from eight seasons in Japan, but also with an air of mystery. First, there was the number of arrows in his quiver. Most big-league hurlers can throw two or three pitches for strikes, while a few have command of four. Matsuzaka, by contrast, reportedly had as many as eight, including a *shuuto*, a late-breaking pitch with a screwball-like action. He was even rumored to throw a gyroball, a trick pitch that many baseball analysts now believe is a myth.

Then there was Matsuzaka's legendary endurance. In recent years, MLB teams have become obsessive about protecting young arms. They count every pitch and strictly regulate the number of innings their prospects throw. Matsuzaka, meanwhile, was throwing 300-pitch bullpen sessions and 130-pitch games and never iced his arm afterwards. He pitched 13 complete games in 2006, more than the entire staff of any major-league team. During eight seasons in Japan, he went the distance 72 times, an otherworldly feat for North American pitchers.

Matsuzaka rocketed to fame in his native land during the 1998 Spring Koshien, a national high-school tournament watched intently by Japanese baseball fans. After tossing a complete-game shutout for Yokohama High School the day before, the teenager pitched all 17 innings in the quarterfinal, then came in from the outfield (where he played when it wasn't his turn to pitch) to get the save the next day as his team overcame a 6–0 lead and advanced to the final. All Matsuzaka did in the championship game was spin a no-hitter with 14 strikeouts. Those miraculous four days generated a buzz among major-league scouts, but Matsuzaka elected to begin his pro career with the Seibu Lions in Japan's Pacific League. In his eight seasons with the Lions he racked up 108 wins (18 of them shutouts) and struck out 200-plus batters four times.

While he pitched in both the 2000 and 2004 Olympics, it was the inaugural World Baseball Classic that put Matsuzaka front and center on the international stage. In his three starts of the tournament, he allowed just eight hits and two runs over 13 innings, winning all three games, including the championship tilt against Cuba. After he won 17 games for Seibu in the 2006 season, his team agreed to make him available to the highest bidder. Under the so-called posting system, North American teams must submit sealed bids indicating how much they will pay simply for the right to negotiate with Japanese free agents. The Yankees offered $33 million and the Mets $39 million, but the Red Sox trumped them all with a bid of $51.1 million. Boston eventually signed the international star to a six-year, $52-million contract.

Matsuzaka largely lived up to the hype during the first half of 2007. He struck out 10 batters in his first start, fanned 10 more in his third, and then put together a six-game winning streak. By the All-Star break he was 10–6 with a 3.84 ERA, and he was baffling hitters by mixing up his fastball, slider, curveball, cutter, splitter and changeup. During one 35-inning stretch, he posted a 1.03 ERA and struck out 43 batters. His second-half performance, however, was far less impressive: 5–6 and a 5.19 ERA. His 201 strikeouts on the season ranked sixth in the AL, but so did his 80 walks, and he coughed up 25 home runs (only eight pitchers allowed more). As for that legendary endurance, Matsuzaka turned out to

pitch much better when he worked on more than the standard four days' rest: when his right arm enjoyed an extra day off, his ERA was almost a run and a half lower. (He has since taken to icing his elbow and shoulder after games and side sessions.)

Dice-K's late-season woes continued early in the playoffs. He couldn't get out of the fifth inning of his first two October starts, though he bounced back with a strong five frames against the Indians in Game 7 of the Championship Series, earning the win that sent the Red Sox to the World Series. He was outstanding over five innings in his Game 3 start in the Fall Classic (he even helped his cause with a two-run single), and when he got into trouble in the sixth, the bullpen and the Boston offense took over to preserve the win. Matsuzaka may still be making adjustments to the way baseball is played in North America, but it seems he's already figured out how to win.

gil MECHE

It was hard to envy Dayton Moore when he became general manager of the Kansas City Royals in May 2006. As a kid in Wichita, Moore had been a die-hard Royals fan whose favorite team won seven division titles in 10 years, capped with a World Series in 1985. Now his heroes were heading toward their fourth 100-loss season since 2002, and it was Moore's job to right the ship. The Royals had made smart moves in drafting Alex Gordon and trading Carlos Beltran and his big paycheck for Mark Teahen and John Buck. What they needed now was a starting pitcher, so Moore went out and found one in the free agent market, signing Gil Meche to a five-year contract worth $55 million.

To say the deal was criticized would be an understatement — some called it the worst free-agent signing ever. After all, in his previous four years with the offensively gifted Seattle Mariners, Meche was 43–36 with a 4.75 ERA. Was it worth breaking the bank for a pitcher with those numbers?

There was no question that Meche's arm was loaded with talent. He was a first-round pick by the Mariners in 1996, and in two partial seasons in 1999 and 2000 he showed flashes of brilliance while going 12–8 with a combined ERA of 4.24. Before spring training in 2001, however, Meche needed surgery to repair a damaged shoulder, and when it didn't heal properly he went under the knife again that October and eventually lost two full major-league seasons to the injury.

Meche was mostly healthy during his final four seasons in Seattle, starting at least 23 games each season, but his performance was mediocre. The Royals saw a ton of potential, however, pointing out that he was still just 28 years old and entering his prime. Perhaps they saw another Chris Carpenter, who had spent several disappointing and injury-prone years with the Toronto Blue Jays (49–50, 4.83 ERA) before the St. Louis Cardinals took a gamble and turned him into a Cy Young winner.

Well aware that he was now under pressure to throw like an ace, Meche was brilliant in his Opening Day start in 2007. Facing Curt Schilling and the Red Sox, he lasted into the eighth inning, giving up a single run in a 7–1 Royals victory. Meche later admitted that he relished his role as the number-one starter. "It does give me a different mindset when I take the mound," he told *Sports Illustrated*. "I know my team has confidence behind me."

Though he struggled with control in the past, Meche kept his walks lower than ever in 2007 (just 2.6 per nine frames), leaving him with enough gas to go deeper into games, and he logged a career-high 216 innings pitched. While keeping hitters guessing with a knuckle-curve and a changeup, Meche also began throwing more cut fastballs, a pitch right-handed hitters have trouble with. He soon learned how difficult it is to win with an offense as bad as KC's, however. In three of his next five outings after the opener, he did not surrender an earned run, yet he managed one victory. By the break he was 5–6 despite a fine ERA of 3.54. In the end, he wound up with 23 quality starts — only four AL pitchers had more — and a career-best ERA of 3.67. His disappointing 9–13 record was the result of the Royals being second-last in runs scored.

Whether Meche was worth what the Royals paid for him is an open question, but it's interesting to compare his performance with that of other pitchers who inked lucrative deals in 2007. Barry Zito, a former Cy Young Award winner, signed for seven years and $126 million with San Francisco and went 11–13 with a 4.53 ERA, the worst season of his career. Jeff Suppan (four years, $42 million) was a mere 12–12 for the slugging Milwaukee Brewers. The Texas Rangers signed Vincente Padilla to a three-year extension worth almost $34 million and were rewarded with six wins and a 5.76 ERA. The Royals have a long way to go before they turn themselves into a contender, but if they can do it, Gil Meche may turn out to look like a bargain.

$ 24.95

GATE 55

SECTION CLUB

SEAT C7

S6FH536

11JULY08

CAREER HIGHLIGHTS

- matched or exceeded his career highs in strikeouts, innings pitched and ERA in 2007
- represented the Royals at the 2007 All-Star Game
- played for Team USA in the 1995 Junior Olympics

55 PITCHER

Gil MECHE

roy OSWALT

HOUSTON ASTROS ◆ NL Central

Roy Oswalt is proof that scouts sometimes need to look in remote places to find exceptional talent. Oswalt grew up in tiny Weir, Mississippi, a town of a few hundred people where he spent summers helping out on his grandfather's watermelon farm. His high school didn't even have a baseball team until Oswalt's father nagged them into forming one. By 1996, while the diminutive righty was attending a community college near his hometown, hardly anyone even knew about him — except for a trio of scouts with the Houston Astros, who encouraged the club to take a flyer with their 23rd-round pick.

Oswalt went 13–4 in Class-A in 1999, but by the end of the season his shoulder was in terrible pain, and he was considering surgery to repair the damage when something bizarre happened. While working under the hood of his truck, Oswalt touched a live wire and got a powerful shock that knocked him out. When he came to, the pain in his shoulder was gone — forever. Some have guessed that the shock may have loosened built-up scar tissue, but to the Astros it must have seemed like divine intervention.

Oswalt debuted with Houston in May 2001, and by June he had won a spot in the rotation. His rookie season was one of the best anyone had seen in years: he was 14–3 with a 1.06 WHIP, 144 strikeouts and only 24 walks. While the right-hander had a mid-90s fastball, his dominance was a result of his control and his ability to change speeds — he even threw two different curveballs, one of which was so achingly slow that it had batters lunging as they hit weak ground balls.

The Astros had a disappointing year offensively in

2002, but Oswalt won 19 games, failing in his last four starts to reach the magic number 20. The following year, he injured his groin on June 11 and made only eight starts the rest of the way, though he still managed to go 10–5 with a 2.97 ERA. With Oswalt healthy in 2004, the Astros went out and acquired Roger Clemens and Andy Pettitte to assemble a lethal rotation. Clemens took home the Cy Young that year, but it was Oswalt who won 20 games, including 12 in the second half as Houston went from last place on July 24 to a wild card berth. Oswalt notched the decisive victory in Game 5 of the Division Series against Atlanta, and the Astros won his start in Game 4 of the NLCS, but the Cardinals rebounded to win the final two games and take the pennant.

Oswalt was the Opening Day starter again in 2005, and with Pettitte and Clemens throwing brilliantly all season, Houston posted the second-lowest ERA in the league. Of their 89 victories, 20 belonged to Oswalt, who was the only pitcher in the majors to rack up back-to-back 20-win campaigns. The Astros repeated as wild-card winners, and Oswalt stepped up again in the playoffs. In the rematch with the Cardinals in the NLCS, he tossed seven innings of one-run ball

to win Game 2, then returned in Game 6 and held the Redbirds to three hits, sending Houston to the World Series for the first time in franchise history. In his only start of the Fall Classic in Game 3, however, he was touched for five runs in the fifth, and the Chicago White Sox went on to win 7–5 in a 14-inning marathon, completing the sweep the following day.

The Astros missed the postseason in 2006 as Pettitte was merely average and Clemens managed only 19 starts. Oswalt, meanwhile, won a team-high 15 games and led the NL with a 2.98 ERA and a strikeout-to-walk ratio of 4.37. He was named to his second All-Star Team and received a 29th birthday gift in August when the Astros granted him a five-year contract extension. Pettitte and Clemens jumped to the Yankees in 2007, leaving Oswalt to lead the staff alone. He was more than up to it, going 14–7 with a 3.18 ERA before soreness in his left side caused him to miss his last couple of starts. Meanwhile the Astros meager offense dragged the team to its worst record since 2000.

Oswalt has won more games since 2001 than any pitcher in baseball, and his career ERA of 3.07 places him behind only Pedro Martinez among active hurlers, and ahead of Greg Maddux, Roger Clemens, Randy Johnson and Johan Santana. Those numbers give him the dubious honor of being the best pitcher never to win a Cy Young Award.

$ 24.95
GATE 18
SECTION CLUB
SEAT R34
D3FR668
3SEPT08

CAREER HIGHLIGHTS

- ranks third among active pitchers with a .675 winning percentage (112–54)

- owns a perfect 4–0 record and a 3.66 ERA in the postseason

- was a member of the USA's gold-medal-winning team at the 2000 Olympics

44 PITCHER

Roy OSWALT

jake PEAVY

44

In Mobile, Alabama, in the early 1990s the only baseball team you could follow on television was the Atlanta Braves. Jake Peavy was a skinny 14-year-old when he watched the Braves' Greg Maddux win his fourth straight Cy Young Award in 1995. A dozen years later, Peavy would win his own Cy Young while anchoring a rotation that included his former hero. By that time, the 42-year-old Maddux was calling Jake Peavy the best pitcher in the game.

The lanky country boy was a lowly 15th-round draft pick in 1999, but he impressed the San Diego Padres not only with his stuff, but with the way he confronted hitters. He threw a fastball in the mid-90s, plus a hard slider and a changeup that could make hitters look silly. Even before turning 20 he had figured out how to mix his pitches expertly, never letting opponents feel comfortable at the plate. By 2002 he was called up to the majors for good.

During his second full season in 2004, Peavy was simply outstanding. Though he was the junior starter in the Padres' rotation, he quickly established his role as the ace. Despite missing six weeks with a forearm injury, he went 15–6, whiffed 173 batters in 166 innings and led the majors with a sparkling 2.27 ERA, becoming the youngest pitcher to lead his league in that category since Dwight Gooden in 1986. Though he didn't often go deep into games, he allowed one run or fewer in 14 of his 27 starts.

The Padres were a mediocre 82–80 in 2005, but that was good enough to win the weak National League West. Peavy didn't lose a game until June and finished the year at 13–7 with a 2.88 ERA and 216 strikeouts to lead the loop. In Game 1 of the the NLDS that year, the Cardinals' big bats roughed him up for eight runs in just over five innings, and St. Louis made short work of the Padres with a three-game sweep.

Peavy battled tendinitis in 2006 and was held to an 11–14 record, though he still struck out 215 batters.

He finished the year strong, winning four games in September, but he struggled again in the playoffs, getting rocked for 11 hits and five runs in the opener of the NLDS against St. Louis. Although no one questioned Peavy's intensity or will to win, he was beginning to earn a reputation as a pitcher who couldn't nail down the big game when his team needed it.

Unfortunately, he was unable to shake that label in 2007, despite putting up the best overall numbers of his career. In late April, he narrowly missed tying Tom Seaver's record of 10 consecutive strikeouts when he fanned nine Diamondbacks in a row and then induced a two-strike check-swing from Eric Byrnes. The first-base umpire ruled the bat did not come around, and Byrnes walked on the next pitch. Peavy went on to strike out 16 batters that game and logged 10 or more K's in eight other starts that year. With a rotation that included rising star Chris Young and free-agent Maddux, the Padres had the lowest ERA in the league.

Things went awry for both the Padres and their ace late in the season. After trailing San Diego for most of the year, the Arizona Diamondbacks had whittled their way to a tie in the NL West, and when the two clubs met on September 5, Peavy volunteered to go to the mound on three days' rest. He promptly allowed eight runs in four innings, and Arizona took over the division lead and did not relinquish it the rest of the way. The surging Rockies then caught the second-place Padres, forcing a one-game playoff to decide who would get the wild card berth. Peavy took the ball again, and this time he surrendered 10 hits and six runs as the Padres lost a heartbreaker in 13 innings.

Peavy nonetheless ran away with the Cy Young Award in 2007. He notched 19 wins against six losses, compiled a 2.54 ERA and struck out a career-high 240 batters, leading the NL in all three categories to capture the pitcher's version of the Triple Crown.

$ 24.95
GATE 67
SECTION UPPER
SEAT R5
B3HL789
24AUG08

CAREER HIGHLIGHTS

- led the NL in strikeouts per nine innings in both 2006 and 2007
- became the fourth pitcher since 1966 to win the NL pitching Triple Crown (2007)
- has struck out 10 or more batters in a game 24 times, the most ever by a Padres hurler

44 PITCHER

Jake PEAVY

brad PENNY

Brad Penny didn't wait long to make an impression when he was traded to the Florida Marlins' organization in 1999. The right-hander had been drafted by the Diamondbacks in 1996 and had two outstanding years with Arizona's Class-A teams, including a 14–5 season that earned him California League MVP honors. After the deal, the Marlins assigned him to the Double-A Portland Sea Dogs, and in his first appearance, he combined with another hurler to throw the first no-hitter in the club's history.

Not yet 22 years old, Penny made his big-league debut with the Marlins on April 7, 2000, and allowed one run through seven innings to earn his first win. In 22 starts that season, he was 8–7 with a 4.81 ERA, and he didn't lose a game after June 28. He began 2001 by winning his first four decisions and ran his streak to 17 consecutive starts without a loss. He was the nemesis of the Montreal Expos, allowing only one run over 30 innings and winning all four of his starts against them.

In 2002 Penny was part of a talented rotation that included A.J. Burnett and Josh Beckett, and the Marlins also boasted a couple of good sluggers in Mike Lowell and Derrek Lee. The club finished four games under .500, but they had high hopes for the following season. After a slow start in 2003, the Marlins went 17–7 in July and 18–8 in September to finish with 91 wins, coming second in the NL East and nailing down the wild card spot. Rookie of the Year Dontrelle Willis, Mark Redmond and Penny each won 14 games, while Beckett and Carl Pavano rounded out a solid quintet of starters who promised to make things interesting in the postseason. Sure enough, the Marlins knocked off the San Francisco Giants — winners of 100 games in the regular season — in the NLDS, though Penny gave up four runs in four innings during his only start. He was roughed up again in Game 1 of the Championship Series against the Cubs, but earned the win in relief in Game 7. That put Florida in the World Series, and it

was there that Penny was at his best. He beat David Wells in the opener at Yankee Stadium, and then returned in Game 5 to limit the Yankees to one earned run in seven innings. Beckett tossed a shutout the next day to give the Marlins their second championship.

At the trading deadline in 2004, Penny was dealt to the Los Angeles Dodgers in a six-player swap that sent catcher Paul Lo Duca, outfielder Juan Encarnacion and pitcher Guillermo Mota to Florida. Penny made his first start for the Dodgers in early August and threw eight scoreless innings, but in his next appearance he had to leave the game with a biceps injury. He was on the DL until late September, and when he returned he promptly reinjured the muscle. Penny rejoined the rotation the following April and threw well all season, though he was the victim of hard luck. Despite a solid 3.90 ERA and nine starts in which he allowed a single earned run, he won just seven games against nine losses.

Penny charged out of the blocks with a dominating first half in 2006, going 10–2 with a 2.91 ERA before the break. Astros' manager, Phil Garner, rewarded him by selecting him to start the All-Star Game in Pittsburgh, and he opened the game by striking out Ichiro Suzuki, Derek Jeter and David Ortiz. Penny tailed off sharply in the final three months of the

season, however, and his second-half ERA ballooned to 6.25. The Dodgers backed into the postseason by winning the wild card berth, but they elected not to start Penny in the NLDS. He made a relief appearance in Game 1, gave up two runs in one inning and was tagged with the loss. The Mets quickly disposed of the Dodgers in three straight.

When Penny had a poor spring training in 2007, there was talk that he might be fighting a lingering injury. When the season opened, however, he had another marvelous first half, winning 12 of 13 decisions and earning a spot on the All-Star Team for a second straight year. Unlike the year before, he continued his hot hand after the break and finished the season with the NL's best record at 16–4, and the third-best ERA at 3.03.

$ 24.95
GATE 21
SECTION CLUB
SEAT G32
A3DC892
16OCT08

CAREER HIGHLIGHTS

- one of only five pitchers to defeat the Yankees twice in the same World Series (2003)
- struck out four batters in one inning (one reached base on a passed ball) on September 23, 2006
- selected to the NL All-Star Team in 2006 and 2007

31 PITCHER

Brad PENNY

C.C. SABATHIA

Almost immediately after C.C. Sabathia began lighting up the American League with his blazing fastball in 2001, baseball pundits were predicting that either his arm or his temper would sideline his career before he could achieve real stardom. And yet, seven seasons later, the lefty has spent only two stints on the disabled list and has become one of the most dominant pitchers in the game. His continued success is a testament not only to his durable arm and his maturity, but also to how well the Cleveland Indians have managed their ace's workload.

Carsten Charles Sabathia grew up in Vallejo, California, in the Bay Area, where he was an outstanding high school athlete. At six-foot-seven, he was tall enough to play basketball, but it was at football and baseball that he excelled. By the time the Indians drafted him in the first round in 1998, his fastball was already in the high 90s, and two years later he was the organization's best pitching prospect.

Heading into 2001, Cleveland had a robust batting order that included Roberto Alomar, Jim Thome and Juan Gonzalez, but their starting pitching looked thin once you got past Bartolo Colon. As a result, the 20-year-old Sabathia was able to win the fourth spot in the rotation and, although he was the youngest player in the AL, he turned out to be the Tribe's most dependable starter. The team was 24–9 when he took the mound, and he posted a magnificent 17–5 record with 171 strikeouts, including three games in which he fanned 11 batters. He allowed the fewest hits per nine innings of any starter in the loop and helped pitch the Indians to their sixth division title in seven years. That October, Sabathia became the youngest pitcher ever to start an ALDS match. He won the pivotal Game 3 to give the Indians the edge in the series, but they dropped the next two to the powerful Mariners.

In his second start of 2002, Sabathia took a no-hitter into the eighth, but he had an otherwise difficult

first half. His ERA was 5.45 on August 1, but he went 7–2 over the final two months to salvage the season. He pitched so consistently in 2003 that only once in 30 starts did he get the hook before the sixth inning. When he started his 100th career game in 2004, Sabathia was only the second Indians pitcher (the other is Hall of Famer Bob Feller) to reach that milestone before turning 24. He had proven his talent and his durability, but his immaturity remained a problem: when the big lefty got into a jam, when one of his fielders booted a ball, or when he disagreed with an umpire's opinion of the strike zone, he could lose his composure.

Since the second half of 2005, however, Sabathia has learned to control both his emotions and his trademark fastball. He was 9–1 with a 2.24 ERA to close out 2005 and pitched extremely well in 2006 despite a mediocre 12–11 record. That season saw him compile a career-best 3.22 ERA and a 1.17 WHIP, third and fourth in the league respectively. His club, however, was a bust. Touted as leading contenders in the AL Central, the Tribe wound up six games under .500 and were never a factor.

That all changed in 2007, when Sabathia had his strongest season to date.

He was 19–7 with a 3.21 ERA, and led all AL hurlers with 241 innings pitched. His control was astounding: he fanned a personal-best 209 and walked a career-low 37, far and away the best ratio in either league. With the surprising Fausto Carmona behind him in the rotation, the Indians went 96–66, tied for the best mark in the majors. That fall, Sabathia edged out Boston's Josh Beckett for his first Cy Young Award.

In the postseason, however, Sabathia was a major disappointment. The Indians scored 12 runs to help him beat the Yankees in Game 1 of the ALDS, even though in five innings he walked six and served up two home runs. Then he was thoroughly outpitched by Beckett in the Championship Series. The Red Sox bombed Sabathia for eight runs in Game 1 as the Tribe lost 10–3, but he still had an opportunity to nail down the pennant when the Indians rebounded to win the next three. In Game 5, however, the Sox knocked him around for 10 hits and four runs in six innings, while Beckett shut down the Indians again. Sabathia would have loved an opportunity to redeem himself in the World Series, but the Bosox completed the comeback in Games 6 and 7, and he never got the chance.

$ 24.95

GATE 40

SECTION CLUB

SEAT V5

U6AB437

9SEPT08

CAREER HIGHLIGHTS

- logged his 100th win and 1,000th strikeout in 2007
- has more wins (100) than any other active pitcher under 28 years old
- his 5.65 strikeout-to-walk ratio in 2007 was the best ever recorded by a left-handed pitcher

52 PITCHER

C.C. SABATHIA

johan SANTANA

MINNESOTA TWINS ◆ AL Central

When Johan Santana was 15 years old, he thought he might like to become an electrician like his dad. Johan played for his local team, the Chiquilines, in the remote town of Tovar, Venezuela, but he didn't think of baseball as a potential career. Then one day an intrepid scout for the Houston Astros rented a car and drove for 10 hours through the Andes to the Santana family home. The scout handed the wide-eyed teenager a baseball autographed by the 1994 Astros and invited Johan to the team's training facility in Valencia. A decade later, American League batters were wishing that scout's car had broken down on the way.

A 16-year-old Santana signed with the Astros following the 1995 draft and spent four years in their farm system, but he was left off the 40-man roster in 1999, which allowed Florida to grab him in the Rule 5 draft. The Marlins immediately dealt him to the Minnesota Twins, who were required to keep him on the major-league roster in 2000. The 21-year-old made five starts and 25 relief appearances that season, posting an unimpressive 6.49 ERA.

The Twins returned Santana to the minors, and in 2002 he was playing with the organization's Triple-A affiliate in Edmonton, Alberta, where a pitching coach helped him develop a deadly new weapon: the changeup. Santana learned to throw it 10 or 15 miles per hour slower than his fastball using the exact same arm motion, and soon had batters so far out in front that their swings looked ridiculous. Back in the majors by the end of May, Santana won seven of his 13 starts, but the Twins used him mostly from the bullpen. He appeared in six postseason contests that year — including the final four games of the ALCS against the Angels — but he was ineffective, allowing six earned runs in just over six innings.

Santana pitched 27 games in relief again in 2003,

but made his case for a spot in the rotation by going 11–2 with a 2.85 ERA in 18 starts, helping the Twins to a division title. Manager Rod Gardenhire even handed him the ball for Game 1 of the ALDS against the Yankees. He was brilliant in the first four innings, but had to leave because of a cramped hamstring. When he valiantly tried to come back for Game 4, the Yankees pummeled him, winning the match and the series.

Santana had offseason surgery to remove bone chips in his elbow, and it hampered his performance early in 2004. But once he was healthy he showed complete control of a late-breaking slider as well as his fastball and devastating changeup. Santana suddenly began to flourish. In the second half he was an astounding 13–0, winning Pitcher of the Month honors in July, August and September — and carried the team to its third straight AL Central title. In one of his most remarkable outings, he outdueled Pedro Martinez, striking out 12 Red Sox and helping the Twins to a key victory. He wound up winning 20 games and leading the AL in WHIP (0.92) and strikeouts, fanning 265 while issuing only 54 walks. Santana pitched seven scoreless innings to lead the Twins to a 2–0 win in Game 1 of the ALDS, but the Yankees swept the next three to take the series. In November, Santana received all 28 first-place votes to take home his first Cy Young Award.

In 2005 and 2006, Santana continued to be the most feared hurler in the league. With supreme command of all his pitches, he allowed less than one base runner per inning in both seasons, won back-to-back strikeout crowns and posted a combined 2.82 ERA. He was 35–13 over the two seasons, including an astonishing 19–3 after the All-Star break. By the end of 2006, his lifetime winning percentage was .716, the second-best in MLB history at the time. He was again a unanimous choice for the Cy Young Award in 2006.

For the first time in his career, Santana had a poor second half in 2007 (5–7, 4.04 ERA), his most disappointing season to date, finishing barely above .500 at 15–13. He still led the AL with a 1.07 WHIP, was second with 235 strikeouts and posted a 3.33 ERA. He logged seven games with 10 or more strikeouts, and on August 19 he fanned 17 Texas Rangers over eight innings in a 1–0 victory. Johan Santana's "disappointing" is, after all, more than most other pitchers can ever aspire to in their best years.

CAREER HIGHLIGHTS

- led the American League in WHIP for four consecutive seasons (2004–07)
- won the pitching Triple Crown in 2006, leading the AL with 19 wins (tied), 245 strikeouts and a 2.77 ERA
- named to three consecutive All-Star Teams (2005–07)

57 PITCHER

Johan SANTANA

$ 24.95
GATE
SECTION 9
CLUB
SEAT G6
T5BN168
15JUNE08

ben SHEETS

Ben Sheets became a national baseball hero before he even threw a pitch in the majors. After spending the 2000 season in the Milwaukee Brewers' minor-league system, manager Tommy Lasorda invited the 21-year-old to join Team USA for the Summer Olympics in Sydney. He turned out to be the staff's ace, surrendering a single run over 13 innings during his first two starts before taking the mound in the final against a heavily favored Cuban squad. Sheets then went out and threw the game of his life on September 27 — a three-hit shutout that gave the United States its first gold medal in Olympic baseball.

Sheets made his big-league debut the following April, and after losing his first two starts, he won 10 of his next 12 decisions. By the end of June his ERA was a tidy 3.34, good enough to make an appearance in the All-Star Game. He struggled in the second half — the Brewers' bats offered little help — and went winless the rest of the way, but he impressed the club enough to be named the Opening Day starter in 2002. Unfortunately, the Brewers were abysmal that season, losing 106 games for the worst record in the NL. Sheets tossed 22 quality starts and posted a decent 4.15 ERA, but the Brewers won only 12 games with him on the mound. In the end, the hard-luck righty came away with an 11–16 record.

Wasted performances soon became routine for the Brewers' number-one hurler. In 2003, despite throwing in pain because of two bulging discs in his back, Sheets led the team with 220 innings pitched, and his 1.8 walks per nine innings was third-best in the league. But again he lost more games than he won with the last-place club. In the offseason he received treatment for his back and worked his upper body hard, and by spring he had bulked up noticeably. Working with pitching coach Mike Maddux, he adjusted his delivery to get more velocity on his fastball. When the 2004 season opened, Sheets was pain-free and his heater had crept into the high 90s. Combine that with what may be the best curveball in the league, and batters were in for a tough time.

As expected, Sheets was dominating in 2004. He threw 24 quality starts, logged an ERA of 2.70 and was second in the league with a stellar 0.98 WHIP. In April he went five straight starts without issuing a walk, while striking out 31. That was a teaser for what he would accomplish on May 16 against Atlanta. In command of all his pitches, Sheets struck out two Braves in each of the first, second and third innings, then fanned another in the fourth and all three in the fifth. He wound up punching out six of the final seven batters he faced for a three-hit, 18-strikeout masterpiece. Sheets finished the campaign with 264 K's and only 32 walks, the best ratio in the majors. His record during this extraordinary season? An ugly and undeserved 12–14, courtesy of a Brewers' offense that was shut out or limited to one run in 10 of his starts.

Sheets has since been slowed down by a slew of injuries. In 2005 he spent time on the DL with an inner ear infection, and then lost two months to a torn upper back muscle, though he still managed a fine 3.33 ERA and became the first Brewer pitcher in more than two decades to win 10 or more games in five straight seasons. The following year he missed much of the first half with a pair of shoulder injuries and played in only 17 games.

After so many years of toiling on a dismal team, Sheets finally had the chance to pitch his team into a postseason in 2007. But the injury bug bit him again — and again, and again. He suffered an early-season groin strain, a sprained finger and a hamstring pull mixed in with his 24 starts. He was ineffective after coming off the DL in late August and the surging Cubs overtook Milwaukee to win the division.

With the slugging Brewers finally giving him some run support, he won 12 games against just five losses in 2007, but in his seven major-league seasons Ben Sheets has compiled a 73–74 record with a 3.83 ERA. That makes him without a doubt the best sub-.500 pitcher in the majors.

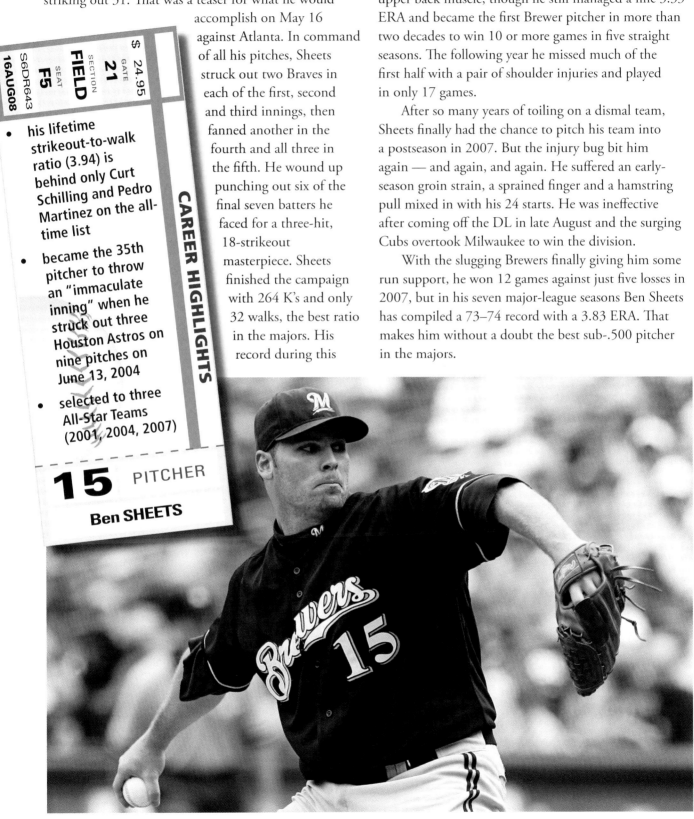

$ 24.95
GATE 21
SECTION FIELD
SEAT F5
S6DR643
16AUG08

CAREER HIGHLIGHTS

- his lifetime strikeout-to-walk ratio (3.94) is behind only Curt Schilling and Pedro Martinez on the all-time list

- became the 35th pitcher to throw an "immaculate inning" when he struck out three Houston Astros on nine pitches on June 13, 2004

- selected to three All-Star Teams (2001, 2004, 2007)

15 PITCHER

Ben SHEETS

john SMOLTZ

ATLANTA BRAVES ◆ NL East

Many pitchers have had success as both a starter and a reliever. But only one has ever gone from Cy Young–winning starter to lights-out closer, and then returned for a second career as an ace. That unique pitcher is the Atlanta Braves' John Smoltz.

Born in a suburb of Detroit, Smoltz was thrust onto the national stage as a 24-year-old in 1991, when he battled his boyhood hero, Jack Morris, in what may have been the most thrilling Game 7 in World Series history. Smoltz threw seven scoreless innings for the Atlanta Braves before leaving in the eighth, while Morris went the distance for a 10-inning shutout to give the Minnesota Twins a 1–0 win and their second championship. That heartbreaker would be the first of a remarkable string of 13 straight trips to the postseason for Smoltz, highlighted by the Braves' World Series win in 1995.

In 1993, Greg Maddux joined Smoltz and Tom Glavine to give Atlanta one of the greatest trios of starters in history. Over the next three seasons Smoltz was the number-three man, but 1996 belonged to him alone. In his third start on April 14, he struck out 13 batters and flirted with a no-hitter, allowing only a double that could

$ 24.95
GATE 1
SECTION
UPPER
SEAT E5
O3SA472
5OCT08

CAREER HIGHLIGHTS

- only pitcher in MLB history to record 200 wins and 150 saves

- all-time leader in postseason wins (15) and strikeouts (194) and has lost just four of 27 playoff starts

- needs 25 strikeouts to become the 16th pitcher to reach 3,000

29 PITCHER

John SMOLTZ

have been ruled an error on his left fielder. That was the second victory in what would stretch into a 14-game win streak. The right-hander completed the campaign with a stellar 24–8 record, a 2.94 ERA and a league-best 276 strikeouts to run away with the Cy Young Award, ending Maddux's string of four in a row.

Smoltz was plagued with elbow problems in 1998 and 1999, and endured four separate stints on the DL. He tried desperately to pitch through the pain, even experimenting with a knuckleball, but ultimately decided to undergo Tommy John surgery which forced him to sit out the entire 2000 season. When he struggled in his first five starts of 2001, manager Bobby Cox decided to move him into the bullpen. That's a move that managers often make as damage control, but Smoltz turned out to be almost unhittable in his new role. In the first 31 relief appearances of his career, he posted a 1.59 ERA and picked up 10 saves.

During the next three campaigns, Smoltz transformed himself into one of the best closers the game has ever seen. He set a National League record in 2002 with 55 saves, including a streak of 25, joining Dennis Eckersley as the second of only two pitchers to record a season with 20 wins and another with 50 saves. From June 3 to the end of that year, the Braves were an unbelievable 49–0 in games that Smoltz appeared in. They also won his first 24 games to start 2003, helping

him set an MLB mark with 34 saves before the All-Star break. He recorded his 100th save in his 151st relief appearance, faster than any pitcher in history; had he not coughed up a pair of runs in his final outing, he would have finished with an ERA under 1.00. When he saved 44 games in 2004, Smoltz became the sixth pitcher to post three straight seasons of 40 or more.

Despite his unqualified success as a closer, however, the Braves did not make it past the first round of the playoffs from 2002 to 2004, and Smoltz strongly believed that he could help the team more as a starter. He pushed hard for the opportunity, but Cox was understandably reluctant. No one had ever won 150 starts, then saved 150 games, then returned to the rotation. Could his 38-year-old elbow go back to throwing 200-plus innings again? Eventually, Smoltz got his way, and he succeeded brilliantly again. In 2005 he threw 229 innings, winning 14 games with a 3.06 ERA. He followed up with 16 wins and 211 strikeouts in 2006.

The 40-year-old was still going strong in 2007 as he led the Braves with a 3.11 ERA and a 4.19 strikeout-to-walk ratio. Early in the season Atlanta signed Smoltz to a contract extension that includes options for 2009 and 2010, depending on whether he can still throw 200 innings. If he can't, who knows, they might just give him another shot as a closer.

justin
VERLANDER

By the end of the 2006 regular season, no one was questioning Justin Verlander's talent. Along with Jeremy Bonderman and Joel Zumaya, his team's other lively young arms, Verlander was a main reason the Tigers were heading toward the World Series after a dozen consecutive losing seasons. The 23-year-old had been the first rookie pitcher to win 10 games before the end of June. But he dropped five of his final eight decisions, and his last outing pushed his innings total to 186 on the year — 67 more than he had ever pitched before. As the Tigers headed to the postseason, they had to wonder whether Verlander's right arm would hold up.

Verlander was Detroit's first-round pick in the 2004 draft, following his three outstanding years at Old Dominion University in Norfolk, Virginia. He'd always had a good heater, and as a college freshman he started a weight-training regimen that added muscle to his six-foot-five frame and tacked a few miles per hour onto his fastball, which was being clocked in the high 90s. After signing with the Tigers, he raced through their minor-league system: in 2005 he was a combined 11–2 with a 1.29 ERA in Class-A and Double-A before being called up to the majors before the season was out.

In spring training of 2006, Verlander threw well enough to win the fifth spot in the starting rotation. In his first outing of the regular season, he gave up two hits over seven scoreless innings, and then won four straight starts in May, including a shutout against the Kansas City Royals. The radar gun occasionally measured his fastball at 100 miles per hour, even late in the game, and his curveball was one of the deadliest in the league. But Verlander's success came as much from his savvy as from his stuff: he thought through each at-bat like a veteran and knew more than one way to get a batter out. (Indeed, his strikeout numbers were relatively low for a young fireballer.)

In August, Verlander admitted that his shoulder was bothering him after his starts, and with the Tigers clinching the wild card berth, his year was about to get longer. By now the fifth starter had been promoted, and he started Game 2 of the ALDS against the Yankees, getting a no-decision after allowing three runs in 5⅓ innings. He beat Oakland in Game 2 of the Championship Series, though his four runs in less than six innings were hardly vintage Verlander. When the Tigers advanced to the World Series, the Cardinals battered him for six runs in five innings in the opening game. He got the start again in the decisive Game 5 and pitched his best game of the postseason, but a pair of unearned runs sank the Tigers and Verlander was tagged with the loss again. In four postseason games, his ERA was 5.82, and many put his spotty performance down to fatigue.

But if Verlander's arm was overworked in 2006, he showed

no sign of it the following season. He did not surrender an earned run in his first two outings, and had won six of eight decisions by June 12, when the Tigers hosted Milwaukee for an interleague game at Comerica Park. Verlander and Brewers starter Jeff Suppan locked horns in a classic pitcher's duel that stood at 1–0 going into the sixth inning. Verlander had not allowed a hit to that point, and fans inched toward the edge of their seats after Magglio Ordonez made a sliding grab of a line drive in the seventh, and the infield turned a nifty double play to erase a one-out walk in the eighth. Verlander needed seven pitches in the ninth to blow away Craig Counsell and Tony Graffanino, the first two batters, leaving only J.J. Hardy to deal with. Verlander quickly got in front 0–2 before Hardy hit a curveball high into right field. It landed harmlessly in Ordonez's glove, and the 24-year-old had his no-hitter — the first by a Detroit pitcher in 23 years.

Verlander proved in 2007 that he can handle a 200-inning workload. In August and September he was 7–2 and finished the season with a stellar 18–6 record, a 3.66 ERA and 183 strikeouts, 59 more than in his rookie season. Unlike so many talented young pitchers who proved to be one-year wonders, Justin Verlander looks to have a long career ahead of him.

$ 24.95
GATE 31
SECTION CLUB
SEAT V5
T6GC941
24MAY08

CAREER HIGHLIGHTS

- named AL Rookie of the Year in 2006
- one of two pitchers to have won Rookie of the Year, played in a World Series and pitched a no-hitter before age 25
- named to the AL All-Star Team in 2007

35 PITCHER

Justin VERLANDER

chien-ming WANG

NEW YORK YANKEES ◆ AL East

Before the 2007 season began, Andy Pettitte returned to the Yankees and rejoined his old teammate Mike Mussina. Then the baseball media was abuzz in May with the news that Roger Clemens would accept almost $19 million to come out of retirement to throw for the Yankees. By the end of the year, the Bronx Bombers had a trio of 200-game winners in the rotation. Meanwhile, a quiet, unassuming and underpaid 27-year-old from Taiwan went out and outpitched all of them. You wouldn't know it from the New York press, but the ace of the Yankees' staff for two years running has been Chien-Ming Wang.

Wang grew up in southwest Taiwan, an island that has produced only four other major-league ballplayers. Wang was primarily a fastball pitcher when New York scouts signed him in 2000, and he began experimenting with a sinker four years later while he was with Columbus, the Yankees' Triple-A affiliate. With that

new weapon in his arsenal, Wang went 5–1 with a 2.01 ERA in 2004 and pitched Chinese Taipei to a 3–0 win over Australia at the Summer Olympics in Athens.

On April 30, 2005, Wang made his major-league debut against the Toronto Blue Jays at Yankee Stadium, and went on to win six games before a shoulder injury at the All-Star break shut him down until September. In his third start back from the DL, he tied a major-league record for assists by a pitcher after inducing nine comebackers in a single game, proof that his sinker was in perfect form. He was able to last at least six innings in all but two of his 17 starts that season, finishing at 8–5 with a 4.02 ERA. Joe Torre gave him the start in Game 2 of the ALDS against the Anaheim Angels, and Wang pitched well, giving up just one earned run before being lifted in the seventh, but the Yankees lost the game, and eventually the series.

Wang's debut season proved that he had not only

the physical tools to pitch in the big leagues, but also a personality that could survive the Bronx. Though he struggled to learn English and rarely spoke to the media, he was unflappable on the mound, showing confidence and an even keel. Still, few people expected Wang to be as successful as he turned out to be in 2006. By June 13, when he combined with the bullpen on a 1–0 shutout over Cleveland, Wang had won seven of his first nine decisions. He never lost two games in a row that season, and after winning his final two starts he owned a 19–6 record and a 3.63 ERA. Johan Santana grabbed all the first-place votes for the Cy Young Award in 2006, but Wang — who tied Santana for the most wins in the league — was second.

A few critics wondered whether Wang was really as effective as his stellar record suggested. He averaged a measly 3.14 strikeouts per nine innings, a red flag for such a young pitcher. Opposing batters hit .277 off him, higher than the league average. But a more careful analysis of his statistics showed that Wang was not simply the beneficiary of lucky bounces and solid defense. About two-thirds of balls put in play off Wang are hit on the ground — off Santana, by contrast, the figure is about 40 percent — a testament to the lively movement of his sinker. Batters make a lot of contact against Wang, but they rarely hit the ball hard: he surrendered only 12 home runs in 218 innings in 2006.

Wang followed up his impressive season with remarkably similar numbers in 2007, going 19–7 with a 3.70 ERA. In one of his finest outings on May 5, he retired the first 22 Seattle Mariners he faced before serving up a home run to Ben Broussard — one of only nine Wang would allow on the year. His final victory clinched the wild card spot for the Yankees, and Wang was handed the ball for Game 1 of the ALDS against the Indians. With his parents and friends on hand to watch, Wang was rocked for eight runs in an ugly 12–3 loss. The Yankees went to their ace a second time in Game 4, only to be let down again as he could not make it past the second inning. Wang was fortunate that there were plenty of other poor Yankee performances in that series to deflect the blame. Sometimes being ignored by the media has its advantages.

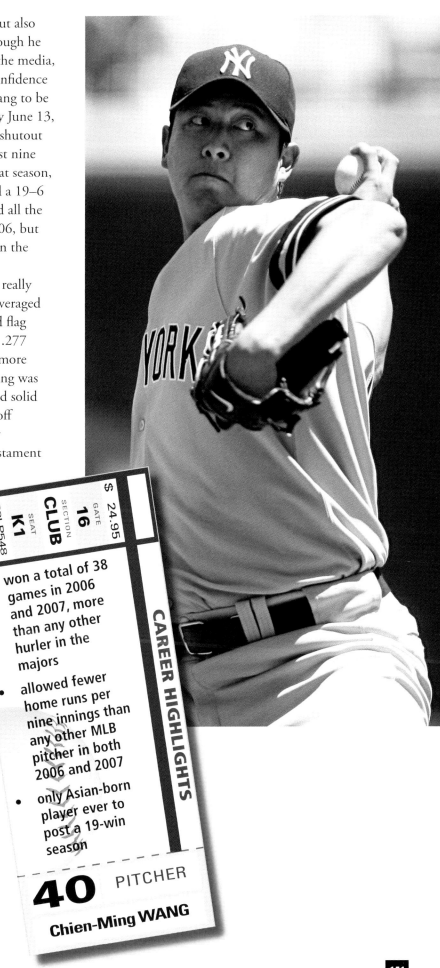

$ 24.95
GATE 16
SECTION CLUB
SEAT K1
P8LP548
30JULY08

CAREER HIGHLIGHTS

- won a total of 38 games in 2006 and 2007, more than any other hurler in the majors
- allowed fewer home runs per nine innings than any other MLB pitcher in both 2006 and 2007
- only Asian-born player ever to post a 19-win season

40 PITCHER

Chien-Ming WANG

brandon
WEBB

Brandon Webb doesn't have the look of an ace — at least not compared with the Diamondbacks hurlers that preceded him in that role: Randy Johnson, who won four straight Cy Youngs with Arizona from 1999 to 2002, and Curt Schilling, who was runner-up in two of those years. Both guys were capable of 300-plus strikeouts a year, and both have a nasty streak. Webb, by contrast, is a ground-ball pitcher who rarely overpowers hitters. He also likes to relax by picking country guitar — he is, after all, from Ashland, Kentucky, the same hometown as Billy Ray Cyrus and Naomi Judd. But don't mistake that laid-back demeanor for a lack of competitiveness. When Brandon Webb is on the mound, he's as tough as they come.

Webb made his first big-league start with Arizona in the opener of a doubleheader in 2003. He threw seven shutout innings, allowing three hits and striking out 10 for his first win. (The D-Backs went on to set an MLB record with 27 total strikeouts in the double-bill after Johnson started the nightcap.) After that debut, Webb tossed 15 more quality starts in a row, an incredible run at the start of a career, and posted a 2.84 ERA — lower than both Schilling's and the Big Unit's.

The Diamondbacks were atrocious in 2004, losing 111 games thanks to the worst offense in the league. Webb contributed 20 quality starts and a 3.59 ERA, but managed to win only seven games, while leading the league with 16 losses. He certainly didn't help himself with an NL-worst 119 walks, but he was also let down by his defense. Webb relies heavily on a two-seam sinking fastball that induces grounders, and the error-prone D-Backs allowed 28 unearned runs during his starts. Still, some baseball analysts predicted that his low ERA was a fluke. *Baseball Prospectus* even called him "an excellent candidate for a complete implosion."

Webb made his critics eat those words in 2005. He improved his control tremendously, walking just 59 batters — half his total from the previous year

— while striking out 172. He began the season 6–0 and ultimately finished at 14–12, a respectable record on a losing club. His sinker was so effective that he recorded 4.34 ground-ball outs for every fly out, the best ratio in baseball by a huge margin — Cleveland's Jake Westbrook was a distant second at 3.13.

Arizona continued its losing ways in 2006, but Webb silenced any remaining doubters with his best season to date. He won his first eight decisions and strung together 30 straight scoreless innings in May and June, and he threw a complete-game one-hitter in September. The pitcher who led the league in walks three years earlier now issued fewer than two free passes per nine innings, and his 1.13 WHIP was second in the NL. Webb's 3.10 ERA would have been impressive enough on its own, but given that he made half of his starts in the hitter's paradise of Chase Field, it was outstanding — indeed, his park-adjusted ERA was tops in the NL. Webb received 15 of 28 first-place votes and edged Trevor Hoffman for the Cy Young Award.

The Diamondbacks improved immensely in 2007, winning 90 games and taking the NL West title. Webb was outstanding again, especially during late July and August. After a pair of seven-inning starts in which he did not allow a run, he went out and threw three consecutive shutouts — the first time a hurler had done that in 10 years — and ran his streak of zeroes to 42 consecutive innings by the time he went to the mound against the Brewers on August 23. The suspense was over quickly: he walked the first batter and later gave up an RBI single to Prince Fielder to end the run. It was the longest scoreless streak since Orel Hershiser of the Dodgers set the all-time mark of 59 in 1988.

Webb closed out the season with a career-high 18 wins and a stingy 3.01 ERA, and then beat the Cubs in Game 1 of the NLDS to lead the D-Backs to a series sweep. The ace got the start in Game 1 of the Championship Series against Colorado, and the Rockies nibbled him to death: their big inning consisted of four singles and a walk. Webb became only the third NLCS starter to lose despite going at least six innings without allowing an extra-base hit.

$ 24.95
GATE 2
SECTION CLUB
SEAT 520
H9TC284
27AUG08
27AUG08

CAREER HIGHLIGHTS

- posted an ERA lower than 3.60 in each of his five seasons and ranks fifth among active pitchers at 3.22
- his 2007 scoreless streak of 42 innings was the fifth longest of all-time
- selected to the NL All-Star Team in 2006 and 2007

17 PITCHER

Brandon WEBB

dontrelle WILLIS

DETROIT TIGERS ◆ AL Central

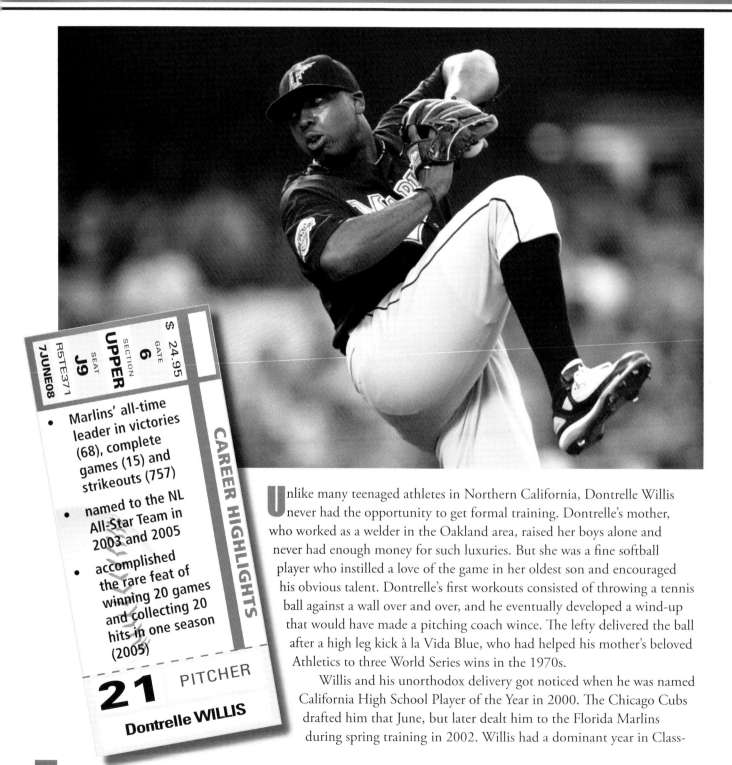

$ 24.95
GATE 6
SECTION UPPER
SEAT J9
R5TE371
7JUNE08

CAREER HIGHLIGHTS

- Marlins' all-time leader in victories (68), complete games (15) and strikeouts (757)
- named to the NL All-Star Team in 2003 and 2005
- accomplished the rare feat of winning 20 games and collecting 20 hits in one season (2005)

21 PITCHER

Dontrelle WILLIS

Unlike many teenaged athletes in Northern California, Dontrelle Willis never had the opportunity to get formal training. Dontrelle's mother, who worked as a welder in the Oakland area, raised her boys alone and never had enough money for such luxuries. But she was a fine softball player who instilled a love of the game in her oldest son and encouraged his obvious talent. Dontrelle's first workouts consisted of throwing a tennis ball against a wall over and over, and he eventually developed a wind-up that would have made a pitching coach wince. The lefty delivered the ball after a high leg kick à la Vida Blue, who had helped his mother's beloved Athletics to three World Series wins in the 1970s.

Willis and his unorthodox delivery got noticed when he was named California High School Player of the Year in 2000. The Chicago Cubs drafted him that June, but later dealt him to the Florida Marlins during spring training in 2002. Willis had a dominant year in Class-

A that season and then won his first four decisions in Double-A in 2003 before the struggling Marlins decided to promote the 21-year-old. When he won his first game on May 14, the club was in fourth place at 19–23, but with Willis' help they turned the season around. From late May to early August he was 10–1 with a 1.87 ERA, and he beat some of the league's top pitchers: he tossed a one-hitter on June 16 to beat Tom Glavine and the Mets, then disposed of Randy Johnson and the Diamondbacks six weeks later with a one-run, eight-strikeout performance. He battled arm fatigue later in the season, but the Marlins played great baseball and overtook the Phillies to secure the wild card spot.

In the postseason, Willis played the triple role of starter, slugger and reliever. In his one start of the Division Series against the Giants he collected three hits, including a triple. Then, after being bombed by the Cubs in Game 4 of the NLCS, he was moved to the bullpen for the World Series and hurled $3^2/3$ innings of scoreless relief as the Marlins knocked off the Yankees. After it was over, the affable young pitcher known as "the D-Train" won Rookie of the Year for his marvelous campaign.

Willis scoffed at the idea of a sophomore jinx after not allowing a run in his first three starts of 2004, but he wore down late in the year, finishing at 10–11 with a 4.02 ERA. He then rebounded with a brilliant season in 2005. Starting strong again, he was 7–0 with a 1.08 ERA in his first seven starts and owned a 13–4 record at the break, earning him his second All-Star selection. His second-half slide was minimal, and he ended the year with an MLB-high 22 wins and a sparkling 2.63 ERA. He threw an MLB-leading five shutouts, the first time a pitcher under 24 had collected that many since Dwight Gooden in 1985. Emerging as one of the best-hitting pitchers in the loop, Willis even chipped in by batting .261, and in his final three games he was slotted seventh or eighth in the lineup — almost unheard of for a pitcher. He finished a close runner-up to Chris Carpenter in the Cy Young voting that fall.

Unlike years past, Willis slumped in the first half of 2006, opening the season at 1–6. But in his final 23 starts he was 11–6 with a 3.39 ERA on a Marlins squad that finished 20 games under .500. Some of his more memorable moments of the year came at the plate at the expense of the Mets: he hit a grand slam at Shea Stadium that was the margin of victory

in a 7–3 July win, and then homered twice off Mets pitchers during a 6–3 triumph in September.

The Marlins had all sorts of pitching woes in 2007 and Willis, surprisingly, was the biggest. In his worst season to date, he allowed more earned runs than any other NL hurler and wound up with an ERA of 5.17 and a 10–15 record. While some have wondered whether all those innings — Willis has never missed a start in five seasons — have burned out his young arm, the Detroit Tigers aren't among the pessimists. Taking advantage of his low stock price, they acquired Willis and teammate Miguel Cabrera in a blockbuster trade in December 2007. Now part of a pitching staff stacked with young talent, the D-Train will look to get back on track in Tigertown.

carlos ZAMBRANO

CHICAGO CUBS ◆ NL Central

Carlos Zambrano has a well-earned reputation for being a hothead. He wears his emotions on the sleeve of his Cubs uniform, and he's been known to mix it up with opponents and teammates alike. But when it comes down to it, Zambrano is as dependable as he is volatile. The big right-hander is a workhorse who has logged over 200 innings for five straight seasons and worked at least six innings in 142 of his 180 career starts. His behavior may be erratic, but his performance on the mound is as consistent as they come.

Zambrano was born in Puerto Cabello, Venezuela, where a Cubs bird dog noticed his rocket arm when Carlos was only 16 years old. Hurlers with his unpolished talent usually need years in the minors to become bona fide prospects, but Carlos was a remarkably quick study, and by age 19 he'd already progressed to Triple-A. His main weapon was a hard sinking fastball; he would later add a split-finger fastball and a slider to his repertoire of pitches, all of which showed lively if unpredictable movement. When he had his best stuff, hitters pounded the ball into the turf. Sometimes, however, his pitches tailed right out of the strike zone and he would walk far too many batters.

After making his major-league debut in 2001, Zambrano spent the first half of 2002 in the bullpen, and then moved into the rotation after the break. By the following season, he was the fourth starter on a top-notch staff, behind Mark Prior, Kerry Wood and Matt Clement. He won 13 games and boasted a 3.11 ERA while tossing a team-high 214 innings and surrendering just nine home runs, the fewest per nine innings in the NL. The Cubs won the Central, and after they dusted off the Braves in the Division Series, Zambrano got the start in Game 1 of the NLCS against the Marlins. His club staked him to a 4–0 first-inning lead, but he blew it by coughing up five runs in the third. Zambrano pitched better in Game 5, but he was outdueled by

Josh Beckett, and the Marlins went on to win the series in seven.

Zambrano worked hard to get into top shape for 2004, which included dropping some extra pounds. The regimen paid off with a fine season: the Big Z went 16–8 with a 2.75 ERA, fourth in the NL and just ahead of the Cy Young–winning Roger Clemens. By now Zambrano was becoming well known for his antics, which included fist-pumping celebrations after key strikeouts, pointing mysteriously at the sky as he walked off the mound, and occasionally plunking batters in situations where it appeared to be intentional. In one infamous game against rival St. Louis, Zambrano was ejected after hitting Jim Edmonds one at-bat after the Cardinals center fielder had admired a home run.

In the following two seasons, as Prior and Wood continually missed starts due to a parade of injuries, Zambrano took over the number-one job. During 2005 he had a 9–0 streak in June and July, struck out 200 batters for the first time, and finished in the NL's top 10 in both ERA (3.26) and WHIP (1.15). Not only was he one of the premier arms in the league, but Zambrano could also help himself with the bat. He hit .300 in 2005 — as a switch hitter no less — and swatted six home runs the next season to win a Silver Slugger. On June 5, 2006, Zambrano hit a three-run homer in the second inning and then took a perfect game into the eighth to beat the Astros almost single-handedly. The Cubs had a terrible 2006, finishing 30 games under .500, yet Zambrano tied for the league lead with 16 wins.

During spring training of 2007, Zambrano made headlines by declaring that he would win the Cy Young Award and the Cubs would take the World Series. Those comments made him look foolish when he was still toting an ERA over 5.00 in early June. So did his actions in his first start that month: after catcher Michael Barrett made two miscues in a five-run inning, the two nearly came to blows in the dugout. During another rough stretch, he ranted against the Wrigley faithful for booing him (he later apologized). Amid those outbursts and slumps, however, Zambrano won 18 games and helped the Cubs catch the Milwaukee Brewers to win the NL Central. His preseason predictions didn't come true in 2007, despite his solid performance in the Division Series against the Diamondbacks, but there's no doubt they're within reach in the future.

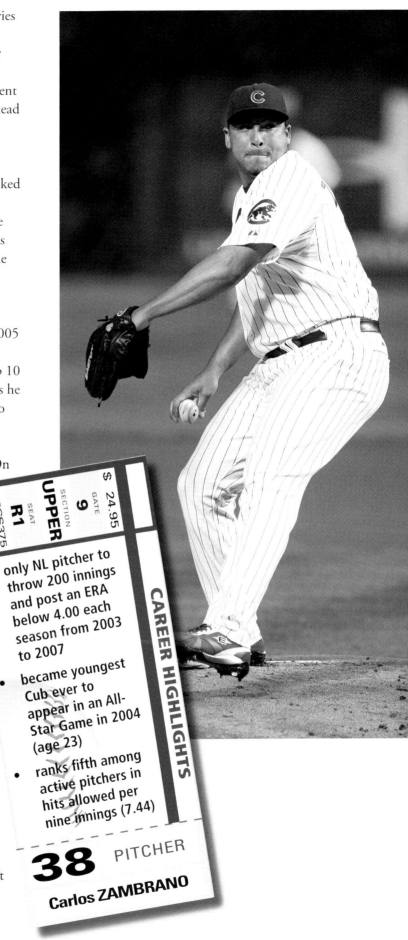

$ 24.95
GATE 9
SECTION UPPER
SEAT R1
N6CS375
26SEPT08

CAREER HIGHLIGHTS

- only NL pitcher to throw 200 innings and post an ERA below 4.00 each season from 2003 to 2007
- became youngest Cub ever to appear in an All-Star Game in 2004 (age 23)
- ranks fifth among active pitchers in hits allowed per nine innings (7.44)

38 PITCHER
Carlos ZAMBRANO

barry ZITO

In the world of sports, where clichés are the usual responses to reporters' questions, Barry Zito is a colorful, quotable alternative. He was born in Las Vegas to musicians who were part of Nat King Cole's band. His family later moved to Southern California, where Barry took up skateboarding, surfing and guitar. While with the A's, he twice danced in *The Nutcracker* to raise funds for the Oakland Ballet. Intelligent, articulate and a little flaky, Zito is not your run-of-the-mill athlete.

Neither was he your typical high-school prospect. The young lefty's chief weapon was an overhand curveball that he could bend into the strike zone with devastating effect. Left-handed hitters, especially, were baffled by it. His fastball was merely in the high 80s, but when batters expected the curve, Zito would surprise them with his four-seamer and punch them out. He did that capably during his year-and-a-half in the Oakland A's farm system, and when he was called up in 2000 he went 7–4 with a 2.72 ERA (the latter was a record for Oakland rookies) in 14 starts. The A's topped the AL West that year to earn their first of four straight postseason appearances, and the 22-year-old Zito made his mark by beating Roger Clemens and the Yankees in Game 4 of the ALDS. The A's lost the series, however, beginning a pattern of outstanding regular seasons followed by early playoff exits.

After a 17–8 sophomore season, Zito was at the height of his dominance in 2002. Oakland's Big Three — which also included Tim Hudson (15–9) and Mark Mulder (19–7) — was the best rotation in the league, and Zito led the trio with an eye-popping 23–5 ledger and a 2.75 ERA. The A's won an amazing 20 consecutive games that August and September, en route to a 103–59 mark and the division title. Barry did his part in the postseason by defeating the Twins in Game 3 of the ALDS, but the A's October woes continued as Minnesota ousted the Athletics in five games. Zito captured the Cy Young Award that fall, squeaking past Pedro Martinez for the honor. At 24, he was the youngest winner since Clemens in 1986.

Zito's roughest campaign came in 2004, when he was 11–11 with a 4.48 ERA (more than a full run higher than any previous season). He had a career-high 13 losses in 2005, but the real story that year was pitiful run support: during those 13 defeats, the A's scored a grand total of 12 runs while he was on the hill. When he received at least two runs from his team's offense, he was 14–2.

The following year was the last of Zito's contract, and the famously low-budget A's had no hope of re-signing him. Perhaps motivated by his impending free agency, he had his best season since his Cy Young campaign, with 16 wins and a 3.83 ERA. His 10 losses, again, were largely due to lack of run support: he was 15–1 when his teammates scored at least two runs for him. The A's again won the West in 2006, and the ALDS began with a classic match-up in which Zito outdueled Johan Santana, leading the way for the A's sweep. This time the disappointment came in the Championship Series. Zito retired the first eight Tigers he faced in Game 1 before surrendering a homer in the third. That opened the floodgates, and by the end of four Detroit had a 5–0 lead that the A's could not overcome. Zito would have started Game 5, but didn't get the chance, as Magglio Ordonez finished off the sweep with a walk-off homer in Game 4.

While agent Scott Boras peddled Zito on the open market that offseason, some baseball analysts suggested that the southpaw's best years were behind him, even though he was 28, an age when many pitchers hit their prime. *Baseball Prospectus* predicted his 2007 totals would be 11–10 with a 4.26 ERA, and that he would post similarly mediocre results over the next four seasons. Nevertheless, Boras convinced the San Francisco Giants that he was worth $126 million over seven years, plus an option for an eighth season at $18 million. The contract remains the biggest of any pitcher in MLB history.

The analysts predictions for 2007 turned out to be optimistic. As "the other Barry" in San Francisco, Zito was a dreary 11–13. Part of that can be pinned on the quiet bats of his last-place club, but his 4.53 ERA was the worst of his career. With six years left on his lucrative contract, Zito, who always has something to say, now has something to prove.

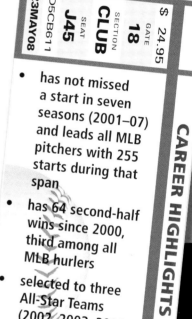

$ 24.95
GATE 18
SECTION CLUB
SEAT J45
D5CB611
23MAY08

CAREER HIGHLIGHTS

- has not missed a start in seven seasons (2001–07) and leads all MLB pitchers with 255 starts during that span
- has 64 second-half wins since 2000, third among all MLB hurlers
- selected to three All-Star Teams (2002, 2003, 2006)

75 PITCHER

Barry ZITO

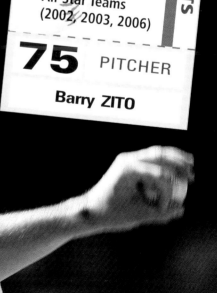

FIREMEN

trevor HOFFMAN

SAN DIEGO PADRES ◆ NL West

Yogurt has a longer shelf life than many closers. Baseball history is filled with relief pitchers who were unhittable for a year or two, and then blew out their arms or crumpled under the pressure. Of the few who remain productive for a decade, many wear out their welcome in half a dozen cities before their careers wind down. And then there's Trevor Hoffman, who has recorded more than 500 saves during 15 seasons with the San Diego Padres.

Looking back, it's difficult to believe that the Cincinnati Reds drafted Hoffman in 1989 as a shortstop. After he batted .212 in Class-A and put one too many throws over the first baseman's head, Hoffman successfully recreated himself as a pitcher. In 1993, the Florida Marlins saw enough promise to take him in the first round of the expansion draft. He made 28 appearances that year before the Marlins traded him to San Diego for Gary Sheffield and journeyman pitcher Rich Rodriguez.

Hoffman recorded 51 saves during his first two full seasons with the Friars, and by 1996 he had built himself into one of the league's best stoppers. He saved 42 of the club's 91 wins that year as San Diego won the NL West. Hoffman failed his first postseason test however, allowing two runs in the ninth inning of Game 3 of the NLDS, enabling the Cardinals to complete their sweep.

Hoffman had his best year in 1998, again helping the Padres to a division title. He converted 53 of 54 save opportunities (only Eric Gagne's perfect 2003 season has been better), allowed two home runs in 73 innings and held opponents to a .165 average. In addition to grabbing the Rolaids Relief Man Award, he finished second in the Cy Young voting and actually received more first-place votes than winner Tom Glavine. It was a remarkable time for the Padres and their closer: on April 28, 1999, when Hoffman finally coughed up a game-winning homer in the ninth, it

ended a run of 181 consecutive games in which the Padres had not lost when leading after eight innings.

Even when San Diego was a mediocre club, National League batters came to dread the sound of AC/DC's "Hells Bells," which rings from the PA system whenever Hoffman jogs in from the bullpen. The Padres finished under .500 each year from 1999 to 2001, yet Hoffman still logged 126 saves, nailing down an amazing 55 percent of his team's victories. Never in possession of an overpowering fastball, the aging closer has learned to rely heavily on his control and on his devastating changeup, still considered one of the best in the sport.

Heading into 2006, Hoffman had 436 career saves and was ready to launch an assault on Lee Smith's record of 478. On August 5, he recorded his 30th of the season to become the first reliever to reach that mark 11 times. Then, on September 24, he threw a perfect ninth against the Pirates in a 2–1 victory for save number 43 on the season and the 479th of his Hall of Fame career. He won his second Rolaids Relief Man Award and was again runner-up for the Cy Young.

The 2007 season was one

of triumph and tragedy for the new all-time saves leader. On June 6, he gave up a leadoff double against the Dodgers, but then set down the next three batters for career save 500. On August 31, he preserved a 6–4 lead against those same Dodgers to give the Padres a share of first place in the NL West. San Diego played .500 ball the rest of the way, however, allowing Arizona to take the division crown and the surging Colorado Rockies to challenge for the wild card spot. Things unraveled for the Padres on September 29 when Hoffman blew a save that would have clinched a postseason berth, setting up a one-game tiebreaker with the Rockies. San Diego looked to have that game locked up after Scott Hairston's two-run homer in the top of the 13th and Hoffman coming in to slam the door. But the Rockies rallied for three straight extra-base hits, and Matt Holliday scored the winning run to send Colorado to the playoffs.

Hoffman accepted responsibility for failing in the clutch, but the veteran knows that one of a closer's most important traits is a short memory. Coming off his fourth straight season of 40-plus saves, he'll be back to add to his all-time save record. Choice of music aside, the bell hasn't yet tolled for Trevor Hoffman.

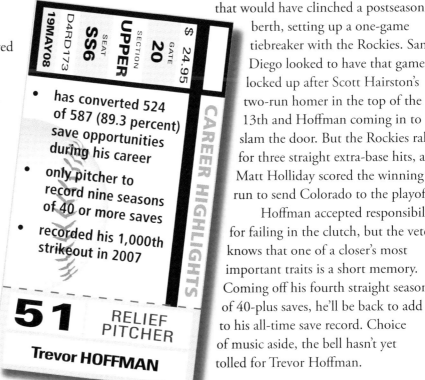

$ 24.95
GATE 20
SECTION UPPER
SEAT SS6
D4RD173
19MAY08

CAREER HIGHLIGHTS

- has converted 524 of 587 (89.3 percent) save opportunities during his career
- only pitcher to record nine seasons of 40 or more saves
- recorded his 1,000th strikeout in 2007

51 RELIEF PITCHER

Trevor HOFFMAN

bobby JENKS

One of the appealing things about baseball is that it offers players a chance at redemption. In 2004 Bobby Jenks' once-promising career was in the tank. The 23-year-old was dealing with a damaged arm and a host of personal problems that finally compelled the Anaheim Angels to give up on him. Less than three years later, Jenks had a World Series ring, two All-Star selections and a share of an extraordinary pitching record.

As a young man, Jenks had problems controling both his fastball and his behavior. He was ineligible to play baseball during three of his four high-school years because of poor grades, though his heater was so impressive that it attracted attention from MLB scouts. The Angels drafted him in 2000, but during the next four seasons, he floundered in the Anaheim organization. He threw hard, but lived harder, and his problems with alcohol prevented him from realizing his obvious potential. After he missed much of the 2004 season with an elbow injury, the Angels placed him on waivers in December.

That's when the Chicago White Sox decided to take a chance on Jenks. They claimed him for $20,000 and sent him to their Double-A affiliate with the idea of turning him into a closer. Jenks thrived in his new role in 2005, and by early July he had earned 19 saves when the White Sox, riding a comfortable lead in the AL Central, decided that he could bolster their bullpen. Chicago's closer, Dustin Hermanson, was having a fine season, so Jenks initially helped out as a setup man and finished games in non-save situations. By the final week of the season, however, as the White Sox' lead had shrunk to two games, it was Jenks who nailed down the division title: he saved three of his team's final four matches, including the clincher.

Jenks suddenly found himself in the postseason as a full-time stopper. He saved Games 2 and 3 in the ALDS as Chicago swept Boston, the defending World Series champs. Then, facing Houston in the Fall Classic, Jenks appeared in all four games. After closing out Game 1, he surrendered a two-run game-tying single to Jose Vizcaino in Game 2 before Scott Posednik won it for the Sox with a walk-off homer. With Chicago looking for a sweep in Game 4, Jenks took the ball in the ninth inning with a 1–0 lead. The Astros threatened with a leadoff single and a sacrifice bunt to put the tying run in scoring position, but Jenks retired the next two hitters to make the White Sox champions. It was the first time in history that a rookie had saved the deciding game in a World Series.

During 2006 Jenks came of age as one of the best closers in the league. In his first full season he saved 41 games in 45 opportunities and allowed just five of 30 inherited runners to score, the second-best rate in the AL. The White Sox won 90 games, but finished third in the strong AL Central, behind Minnesota and Detroit. The following season was miserable for Chicago, and they were already out of serious contention by May. Jenks had 24 saves at the break to earn his second straight All-Star selection, but baseball insiders were murmuring that he had lost several miles per hour off his fastball, which had once routinely been in the high-90s. A frustrated Jenks refused to discuss the subject except to argue, quite rightly, that he was still getting batters out.

By July 2007 most of the baseball media were preoccupied with Barry Bonds' pursuit of the all-time home run record. When Bonds finally hit number 756 on August 7, few noticed that Jenks had not allowed a baserunner in his last 10 outings. Three days later, he had pushed the streak to 35 consecutive batters and was within striking distance of the AL record of 38. He matched that with a one-two-three ninth inning against Seattle, and then closed out the Mariners again on August 12 to tie the major-league record of 41. Fans had to wait a week to see if he could set a new mark, as Jenks nursed a sore ankle. When he returned to the mound against the Royals on August 20, he gave up a single to the first batter he faced, ending a marvelous string of almost 14 perfect innings.

Jenks reached the 40-save plateau in 2007 for the second straight season. As he aims to help the 2008 White Sox rebound from their worst campaign since 1995, it's clear that the move to the bullpen that resurrected Jenks' career was the biggest save of them all.

$ 24.95
GATE 13
SECTION FIELD
SEAT B57
G2DE672
2SEPT08

CAREER HIGHLIGHTS

- owns AL record for most consecutive batters retired (41)
- one of three pitchers to record 40 saves in his second big-league season
- named to the AL All-Star Team in 2006 and 2007

45 RELIEF PITCHER

Bobby Jenks

joe NATHAN

MINNESOTA TWINS ◆ AL Central

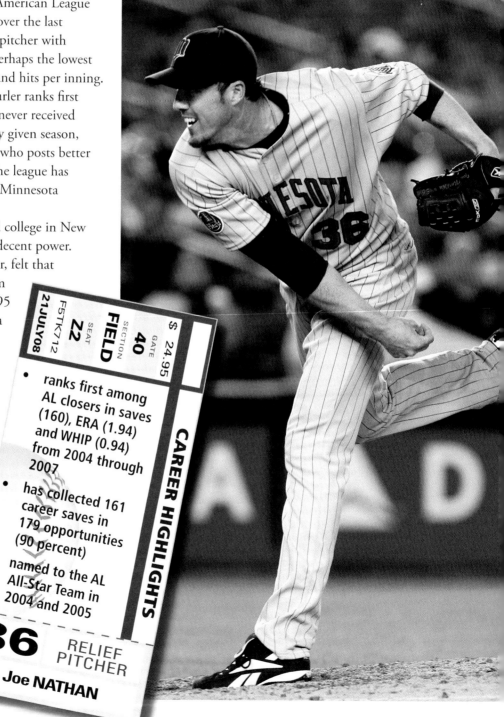

How would you determine which American League closer has been the most reliable over the last four seasons? You might look for the pitcher with the most saves during that span, or perhaps the lowest combined ERA, or the fewest walks and hits per inning. Now, what if we told you that one hurler ranks first in all three of those statistics but has never received the Rolaids Relief Man Award? In any given season, there always seems to be one stopper who posts better numbers, but since 2004 no one in the league has been as consistently dominant as the Minnesota Twins' Joe Nathan.

Nathan attended high school and college in New York, where he was a shortstop with decent power. Scouts who watched Nathan, however, felt that his six-foot-four frame and strong arm had more promise as a pitcher. In 1995 the San Francisco Giants selected him in the sixth round and sent him to their Class-A affiliate in Bellingham, Washington, where he batted .232 with three home runs. Discouraged, he took the next year off to complete his college degree, and when he returned to baseball the Giants worked on turning him into a pitcher. Two years later, on April 21, 1999, he made his major-league debut, tossing seven shutout innings in a 4–0 win over the Florida Marlins.

During the next three seasons, Nathan bounced between the minors and the big leagues as he nursed a shoulder injury that threatened his career. He made the Giants' rotation

$ 24.95
GATE 40
SECTION FIELD
SEAT Z2
F5TK712
21JULY08

CAREER HIGHLIGHTS

- ranks first among AL closers in saves (160), ERA (1.94) and WHIP (0.94) from 2004 through 2007
- has collected 161 career saves in 179 opportunities (90 percent)
- named to the AL All-Star Team in 2004 and 2005

36 RELIEF PITCHER

Joe NATHAN

out of spring training in 2000, but spent all of the following year and most of 2002 rehabbing on the farm. The Giants decided to try Nathan as a middle reliever in 2003, and the experiment was a rousing success. He appeared in 78 games that season and racked up an impressive 12–4 ledger with a 2.96 ERA. With Nathan's value at its peak, however, the Giants made an ill-advised trade: they shipped him to Minnesota along with Francisco Liriano and Boof Bonser. In return, they acquired catcher A.J. Pierzynski, who lasted all of one year in San Francisco.

The Twins' plan for 2004 was to turn Nathan into a closer to replace Eddie Guardado, who had departed for Seattle. They could hardly have expected him to embrace the new role so completely: from April 15 to June 4, Nathan made 20 appearances without surrendering a run, earning a win and 14 saves. By the midway point of the season, the right-hander was sporting a 1.13 ERA and was selected to his first All-Star Team. He finished with 44 saves in 47 chances, including a club-record 27 in a row — remarkable numbers for a first-time stopper. The division-winning Twins faced the Yankees in the ALDS that October, and Nathan saved Johan Santana's brilliant 2–0 win in Game 1. However, with his club up 6–5 in the 12th inning of Game 2 and looking to take a stranglehold on the series, Nathan walked two batters, gave up a game-tying double to Alex Rodriguez and took the loss when Hideki Matsui's sacrifice fly plated the winner.

Minnesota dropped the next two matches and bowed out in the first round.

Nathan put together several more impressive streaks in 2005, including 15 scoreless appearances to open the season (he had 10 saves and a 0.00 ERA on May 10) and 19 consecutive shutout innings in July and August. He wound up converting 43 of his 48 opportunities and proving that his 2004 season owed nothing to beginner's luck. With a fastball in the high-90s and a punishing slider to go with it, Nathan even drew comparisons with Goose Gossage.

Though his save total dropped to 36 in 2006, the season was in many ways the best of Nathan's career. He won seven decisions without a loss, and blew just two save opportunities. In full command of his fastball and slider, he fanned a personal-best 95 batters in only 68 innings, posted a 1.58 ERA and a minuscule WHIP of 0.79.

Joe Nathan showed no sign of slowing down in 2007, saving 37 of 41 opportunities and keeping his ERA under 2.00 for the third time in four years. When it came to the hardware, however, Nathan went home empty handed yet again: after being overshadowed by Francisco Rodriguez and Mariano Rivera for three seasons, Nathan played second fiddle to the Mariner's J.J. Putz this time. The Twins, of course, picked up his option for 2008 and will look to sign him to a longer-term deal for the future. One of these seasons, the most consistent closer in the league may just get his due.

jonathan PAPELBON

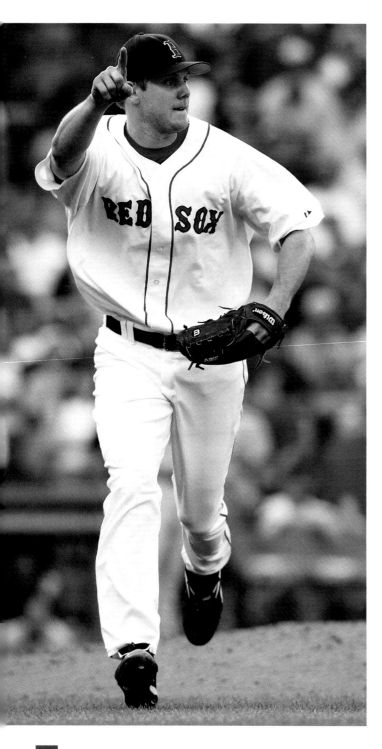

For Red Sox fans, the defining image of the 2007 postseason will always be the dance. While celebrating on the Fenway infield after Boston clinched the AL East, the cameras caught Jonathan Papelbon dancing an Irish jig while clad only in a T-shirt and Spandex shorts. When the Sox won the pennant a few weeks later, he performed his postgame footwork again. And when the team won it all, Papelbon donned a kilt for the World Series parade and did his victory dance on a flatbed truck as it rolled through Beantown.

Jonathan Papelbon's route to the World Series would have been hard to predict two years earlier. Drafted in 2003, the hard-throwing star from Mississippi State University had been both a starter and a closer, but the Red Sox decided to groom him for the former role. Papelbon made his major-league debut as a starter in July 2005 before being shifted to the bullpen later in the season, finishing with a 2.65 ERA in 34 innings.

When spring training began in 2006, it wasn't clear what Papelbon's job would be. Keith Foulke, one of the playoff heroes of 2004, had undergone surgery in the offseason, but he was set to return to the closer's role. Boston's starting rotation was strong as well, so the plan on Opening Day was to use Papelbon as a setup man. That lasted all of one outing, however, and in the third game of the year the 25-year-old earned his first career save with a perfect inning against Texas. He added two more saves in the next series, and by the end of April he had not allowed an earned run. Using a toxic mixture of fastballs in the high-90s, sliders and splitters, he continued to mow down batters before finally blowing his first save opportunity on June 9. When the All-Star break came around, Papelbon had a microscopic 0.59 ERA.

As September dawned, the rookie had compiled 35 saves and seemed a sure bet to break Kazuhiro Sasaki's record of 37 by a first-year pitcher. But on the first day of the month, he felt soreness in his shoulder during a game against the Blue Jays and left after facing three batters. That would be the end of Papelbon's magnificent season, which featured a 0.92 ERA, a 0.78 WHIP and 75 strikeouts in 68 innings.

The shoulder was completely healthy to start 2007, and with the addition of Daisuke Matsuzaka to the starting rotation, Papelbon's role would be closer once again. He opened the season with eight saves in April and added 18 more in the first half to earn his second straight All-Star selection. For the rest of the regular season, Papelbon was remarkably consistent and blew just three save opportunities. With Hideki Okajima as the setup man (the rookie left-hander racked up 26 holds) and Papelbon throwing the ninth, the Red Sox rarely lost in the late innings as they cruised to a 96–66 record and the AL East title.

Facing the Angels in the Division Series, Papelbon came on in the eighth with the score tied 3–3 and escaped unscathed despite an error, a walk and three stolen bases. Then he induced three popups in the

ninth, setting the stage for Manny Ramirez's mammoth walk-off homer in the bottom of the frame. In the ALCS against the Indians, Papelbon made two scoreless appearances early in the series and then entered Game 7 with the Sox up 5–2. He recorded the final six outs to send Boston to the World Series for the second time in four years.

Papelbon saved his best stuff for the Fall Classic. In Game 2, with the Red Sox up 2–1 in the eighth, the Rockies' Matt Holliday singled to put the tying run on base, but Papelbon promptly picked him off to end the inning. He then worked a one-two-three ninth to earn the save. He closed out the third match as well, and then found himself in the pressure cooker of Game 4 the following night. Okajima got the hook after surrendering a two-run homer to Garrett Atkins in the eighth, and Papelbon trotted out to protect a 4–3 lead. After finishing the eighth and retiring the first two batters in the ninth, all that stood between Papelbon and his first World Series ring was pinch hitter Seth Smith. When the Rockies outfielder swung through a 2–2 fastball, Papelbon leaped off the mound and embraced catcher Jason Varitek — and the dancing continued.

J.J. PUTZ

20

J.J. Putz was having a tough week. It was early in the 2005 season and the 28-year-old righty was toiling as a setup man for the Seattle Mariners. Facing the Red Sox on May 14, Putz came on in the seventh with the M's up 3–2 and the bases loaded. He struck out Manny Ramirez, but Trot Nixon ripped his second pitch into the right field seats for a grand slam. Two days later against the Yankees, Putz got a chance to redeem himself in the same situation: Seattle led by a run in the seventh when New York loaded the bases. This time Bernie Williams jumped on Putz's first pitch for another game-winning slam.

After that second blow, Mariners' closer Eddie Guardado was the first to offer consolation. The veteran was always quick to share his experience and advice with his friend, and in spring training of 2006, Guardado even showed Putz how to throw a split-finger fastball. Two months later, and less than a year after his

week from hell, Putz used his devastating new splitter to take over Guardado's job as the Mariners' closer.

Joseph Jason Putz — it's pronounced "puts," as in "puts the ball where they can't hit it" — was drafted by the Mariners in 1999 and was never a top-shelf prospect. After a 12–6 year as a starter in Class-A in 2000, he never posted another winning season in the minors, though he pitched well when moved to the bullpen. By 2004 he was a regular in the Mariners' relief corps and picked up nine saves in 54 appearances that season. The following year his role was to handle the seventh or eighth innings to set the table for Guardado, a two-time All-Star who logged 36 saves in 2005. Putz did well enough in that capacity, with 21 holds and a 3.60 ERA, but no one pegged him to have a breakout year in 2006.

Coming out of training camp that spring, the Mariners figured to stick to the previous year's formula. But Guardado had all kinds of trouble in the early going: he blew three of his first seven save opportunities, and on May 3 he was 0–2 with an ERA of 8.38. Manager Mike Hargrove decided to give Putz an opportunity to close. By early July, the former setup man was throwing his new splitter with lethal consequences. Over his first 22 appearances in the new role, Putz saved 13 straight opportunities, struck out 32 batters, held the opposition to a .171 average and did not give up a single homer. By the All-Star break, Guardado had found a new home in Cincinnati.

Putz continued firing bullets throughout the second half of 2006, saving 20 more games to finish with 36. Most impressive of all was his control: he walked just 13 batters while fanning 104 in 78 innings. During the offseason the Mariners signed their closer to a three-year contract, but then got a scare when Putz injured his elbow during spring training. It turned out to be a mild strain that cleared up with

rest, however, and he was ready to go on Opening Day.

The Mariners started 2007 slowly with a 10–10 record in April, but by midseason they were gearing up to take a run at the division-leading Angels. Putz led the way in June by going 11-for-11 in save opportunities and compiling a 0.59 ERA in 13 games, good for AL Pitcher of the Month honors. At the break his numbers were otherworldly: 24 saves in as many chances, a 0.88 ERA, 44 K's in 41 innings and an opponents' batting average of .129. That was more than enough to earn him a place on the All-Star Team, but ironically, he failed to earn a save in the Midsummer Classic after coughing up a two-run homer to Alfonso Soriano with two outs in the ninth. (The AL hung on for a 5–4 win, with Francisco Rodriguez getting the final out.)

On July 20 Putz set down the Blue Jays in the ninth to preserve a 4–2 lead and notch his 29th consecutive save, a franchise record. Before a rough outing on August 1, he actually had more saves than baserunners allowed, something only Hall of Famer Dennis Eckersley has ever accomplished over a full season. The M's fell apart in late August and early September, but their closer wasn't the problem. Putz blew only two opportunities in the second half and finished with 40 saves to go along with a 6–1 record, a 1.38 ERA and a 0.70 WHIP. All of that added up to his first Rolaids Relief Man Award — and probably not his last.

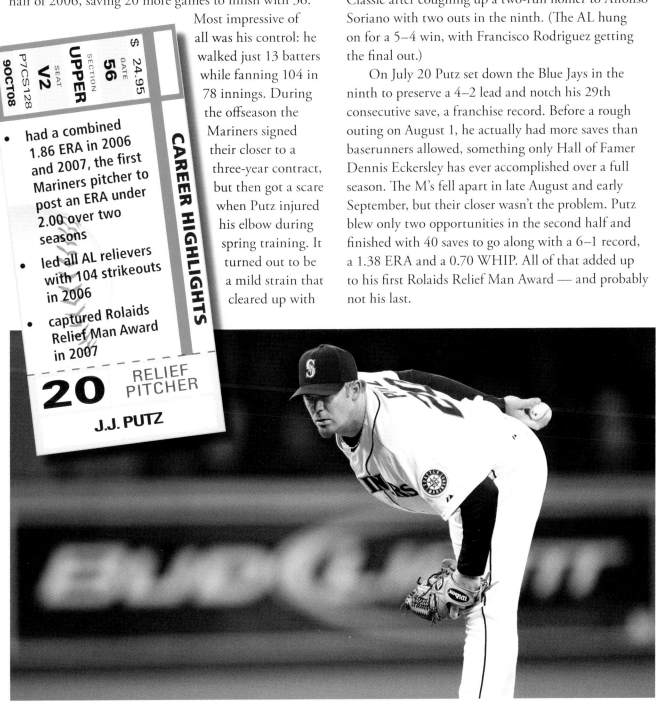

$ 24.95
GATE
56
SECTION
UPPER
SEAT
V2
P7CS128
9OCT08

CAREER HIGHLIGHTS

- had a combined 1.86 ERA in 2006 and 2007, the first Mariners pitcher to post an ERA under 2.00 over two seasons

- led all AL relievers with 104 strikeouts in 2006

- captured Rolaids Relief Man Award in 2007

20   RELIEF PITCHER

J.J. PUTZ

mariano RIVERA

Mariano Rivera once told a sportswriter that his cut fastball was a gift from God. For more than a dozen seasons, however, opposing batters have considered it a curse from the devil. Yes, the legendary closer known as Mo can throw a standard four-seam fastball and the odd changeup, but he is perhaps the American League's most successful one-trick pony. Hitters know the cutter is coming, but they're still helpless as it breaks several inches to the left as it crosses the plate, leaving a forest of broken bats in its wake.

Rivera's career with the Yankees began unremarkably as a starter in 1995. The following season, he worked as a setup man for John Wetteland and was so successful (130 strikeouts, 2.09 ERA) that he placed third in the Cy Young voting. When Wetteland became a free agent in the offseason, the Yankees let him go to Texas and moved Rivera into the closer's role. He struggled there at first — he blew three of his first six save opportunities — but went on to record 43 saves and a 1.88 ERA in 1997. In the ALDS that October, however, he coughed up a game-tying homer to Cleveland's Sandy Alomar in the eighth inning of Game 4. That blow turned the tide, and the Indians won that game and the next two to take the series. Rivera would have plenty of opportunity to atone for that misstep.

In 1998 and 1999, Rivera made it three straight seasons with an ERA under 2.00, logging 36 and 45 saves respectively. The Yankees steamrolled through the postseason and captured the World Series in both years. Rivera was simply magnificent in the playoffs: he did not allow an earned run in 25 ^{2}/$_3$ innings and saved 12 of New York's 22 victories, earning World Series MVP honors in 1999. When the Yankees made it three in a row in 2000, Rivera added six more saves. Indeed, it's Rivera's October dominance that has made him arguably the best closer in the history of the game. He currently ranks third in career saves behind Trevor

Hoffman and Lee Smith, but neither of those hurlers can claim his postseason success: in 76 appearances he logged 34 saves (both MLB records that won't be broken in the foreseeable future) and is 8–1 with a 0.77 ERA.

Ironically, Rivera's two greatest regular-season save totals — 50 in 2001, and 53 in 2004 — were followed by his lowest October moments. His only postseason defeat came in Game 7 of the 2001 World Series against Arizona, when Luis Gonzalez's soft liner went over the drawn-in infield and plated the winning run in the bottom of the ninth. Rivera also blew three save opportunities in the 2004 postseason, most famously in Games 4 and 5 of the ALCS against the Red Sox. (In the fifth match, he merely allowed an inherited runner to score on a sacrifice fly.) Boston went on to win both games in extra innings, setting the stage for their eventual World Series triumph.

The grief Rivera suffered from those heartbreakers seemed to linger into 2005. The Yankees and Red Sox met again in a season-opening series and Rivera blew saves in his first two appearances. But anyone who thought he had lost his nerve was soon proven wrong. Rivera did not fail in another save opportunity until mid-August, at one point nailing down 31 in a row, and finished the year with 43 saves and a stunning 1.38 ERA, the best mark of his career. It was only the third time in MLB history that a pitcher had worked

75 innings, collected 40-plus saves and recorded an ERA under 1.50, and the performance earned him his fourth Rolaids Relief Man Award. The following year his ERA was under 2.00 again, the seventh time he had accomplished the feat.

Rivera's 2007 season was decidedly mediocre by his standards: a 3.15 ERA and 30 saves for a team that won 94 games. At 37 years old, Mo's best years are likely behind him, but his importance to the Yankees goes far beyond his performance on the mound. His long-term success is due not only to his talent and ability to avoid serious injury, but also to his unflappable character, a quality that his teammates regularly praise. Even after the organization dumped Joe Torre at the end of the season, they reached out to Rivera with a three-year, $45-million dollar offer to keep him off the free agent market. The deal may keep him the Bronx until the end of his career — after which it will move to Cooperstown.

$ 24.95
GATE 33
SECTION CLUB
SEAT S3
14JUNE08
U7XE400

CAREER HIGHLIGHTS

- American League's all-time leader in saves with 443
- all-time leader with 34 postseason saves, more than twice as many as any other pitcher
- earned eight All-Star selections and has saved three All-Star Games

42 RELIEF PITCHER

Mariano RIVERA

francisco RODRIGUEZ

LOS ANGELES ANGELS ◆ AL West

The Angels' Francisco Rodriguez is the only pitcher in history to win five postseason games before recording a decision in the regular season — and it's a good bet that the record will never be broken. In the years since that unique feat however, the hero of the 2002 playoffs has ensured he won't simply be remembered as the answer to a trivia question. Still in his mid-20s and already the owner of 146 saves, Rodriguez may be the best young closer in baseball.

Rodriguez grew up in poverty in Caracas, Venezuela, where he was raised by his grandparents after his mother and father walked out on him and his siblings. Baseball was an escape for young Francisco, who started pitching when he was seven years old. He was pushing 90 miles per hour by his mid-teens, and he signed with the Angels in 1998, a few months before turning 17. By 2002, he had developed a sharp-breaking slider to go along with his mid-90s fastball and in mid-September the Angels called him up from Triple-A for a look. In five appearances, he faced 21 batters and struck out 13 of them. The nickname "K-Rod" was born.

When the Angels locked up the wild card berth that year, they kept the 20-year-old on the postseason roster as a fill-in for the injured Aaron Sele. It was a gamble on the part of manager Mike Scioscia. After all, the playoffs aren't just about talent, they're about composure. How would a kid with 15 days of major-league experience survive the pressure cooker? Things began inauspiciously when, in Game 2 of the ALDS against the Yankees, he blew a 4–3 lead by giving up a two-run homer to Alfonso Soriano in the sixth inning. Instead of falling apart, however, Rodriguez brushed himself off and retired the next four batters. When the Angels countered with back-to-back homers of their own in the eighth, he wound up getting the win. He returned in Game 4 to retire six straight Yankees, fanning four of them, to notch the victory again. When

Anaheim advanced to the ALCS, Rodriguez won Games 3 and 5 by pitching 4$^1/3$ scoreless innings and having the good fortune of entering close battles just before the Angels' offense rallied. The next stop was the World Series.

Rodriguez was simply brilliant in Game 2, hurling three perfect frames against the Giants as the Angels' staged a comeback highlighted by Tim Salmon's two-run homer. The victory made Rodriguez the youngest pitcher ever to win a game in the Fall Classic. Overall in the 2002 postseason, Rodriguez was 5–1 with a 1.93 ERA and 28 strikeouts — shattering the old reliever record of 18 playoff K's. And after all that, he was too young to drink the champagne.

The next two seasons were an apprenticeship for Rodriguez. In 2003 he pitched mostly in middle relief, going 8–3 with a 3.03 ERA. The following season, K-Rod stepped in to replace stopper Troy Percival when the veteran was injured, and wound up with 12 saves, a 1.82 ERA and 123 strikeouts — the latter mark is a franchise record for relief pitchers. He had fashioned one of the best two-pitch combinations in all of baseball, regularly getting ahead in the count with his fastball and then using his slider as the *coup de grâce*. Rodriguez's postseason charm wore off in 2004, though. He allowed a mere two runs in 4$^1/3$ innings in the ALDS against the Red Sox, but was tagged with two losses in the three-game sweep.

When Percival jumped to the Tigers in 2005, Rodriguez assumed the mantle of full-time closer for the Angels. He was outstanding in his new role, saving 45 games to tie for the American-League lead. He followed next season with a major-league-best 47 saves in 51 chances, ending 2006 by allowing three earned runs in his final 48 outings and edging out Mariano Rivera for the Rolaids Relief Man Award.

Rodriguez posted his third straight 40-save season in 2007, although his 2.81 ERA was more than a full run higher than the year before. He was thrust onto the October stage again when the Angels captured the AL West crown and faced the Red Sox in a rematch of 2004. Rodriguez's only appearance came in Game 2 in the bottom of the ninth with a runner on and the score deadlocked 3–3. After striking out Kevin Youkilis and walking David Ortiz intentionally, he served up a tape-measure blast to Manny Ramirez that ended the game.

Playing on a perennial contender, Francisco Rodriguez will likely have many more playoff opportunities in his future. He'll be looking to prove that his 2002 heroics were not just beginner's luck.

billy WAGNER

NEW YORK METS ◆ NL East

Being an effective closer requires a combination of physical tools and mental toughness. One look at Billy Wagner's size, generously listed as five-foot-eleven, and you might think it impossible that he could throw a 100-mph fastball — but you would be wrong. As for his ability to deal with ninth-inning pressure, that has never been in doubt. Wagner has faced enough adversity in his personal life to make a blown save look like a tiptoe through the tulips.

The hardship started for Billy when his parents split and he shuttled between his mother's and father's homes, finally settling with an aunt and uncle when he was 15. A natural righty, he suffered a badly broken right arm as a child and learned to throw with his left instead. He practiced — and worked out his frustrations — by hurling pitch after pitch at a cement wall. By the time he reached college, his heater was so lively that the Houston Astros saw past his small stature and chose him in the first round of the 1993 draft.

Wagner was a starter in the minors, and by the middle of 1995 he looked ready for a chance in the big leagues. But the day after he was added to the Astros' 40-man roster, tragedy struck: his wife's father and stepmother were shot dead during a domestic dispute. The terrible event overshadowed whatever pleasure he derived from his major-league debut, which came that September.

In the offseason, the Astros debated whether to add the young fireballer to the rotation or use him out of the bullpen. The problem was that his changeup and curveball were too inconsistent for a starter, though his fastball could be almost unhittable. It took a while for Wagner to find his footing as a reliever, but he was settling into the closer's role in 1998 when fate intervened again. On July 15 the Diamondbacks' Kelly Stinnett turned on a fastball and lined it right back at Wagner — the ball struck him on the left side of the head and knocked him senseless. Amazingly, he returned

CAREER HIGHLIGHTS

- set major-league record of 14.4 strikeouts per nine innings in 1997, then broke his own mark in 1999 (15)

- has held opponents to a .190 average over his 13-year career

- ranks seventh (third among active pitchers) with 358 career saves

13   RELIEF PITCHER

Billy WAGNER

after only three weeks. With help from fellow lefty Randy Johnson, Wagner finally developed an effective second pitch in 1999: a hard-breaking slider. The result was a season that ranks among the best ever by a closer. He fanned 124 batters in under 75 innings and allowed only one run in the final two months to finish the year with a 1.57 ERA and a 0.78 WHIP.

Following season-ending elbow surgery in 2000, Wagner had three more brilliant seasons in Houston. In 2001 he saved 39 of 41 opportunities, and two years later he set a club record with 44 saves, striking out 105 in 86 innings and posting a 1.78 ERA. The Astros, however, could only flirt with greatness. Wagner's tenure included four first-round exits in the postseason, and after the 2003 campaign the outspoken closer publicly questioned the organization's will to win. The Astros, with heir apparent Brad Lidge waiting to take over, responded by trading Wagner to the Phillies.

Unfortunately, he encountered the same situation in Philadelphia. He contributed two outstanding seasons, but angered teammates when he criticized them for what he saw as a lack of desire. When he became a free agent after the 2005 season, he jumped ship again, this time signing a four-year, $43-million deal with the Mets.

Wagner's 40 saves during his first year in New York were the second-best total of his career, and the Mets surprised everyone with a division title. That October, after he saved the first two games in a Division Series sweep of the Dodgers, Wagner finally had the opportunity to pitch in the NLCS. But he was slapped with the loss after giving up three runs in the ninth inning of Game 2, and the Cardinals went on to eliminate the Mets in six.

The Mets and Wagner looked set to take another stab at a championship in 2007: the closer earned his fourth All-Star selection with a huge first half (17 saves and a 1.64 ERA) and the club was sitting atop the NL East at the break. But Wagner battled back spasms late in the season and over the final two months his ERA was 4.88. His last save came on September 12, and he wasn't available to come to his club's aid as they dropped six of their last seven games to surrender the division title to his former team, the Phillies. Billy Wagner has endured far worse setbacks in his life, but that one still had to sting.

Rough
DIAMONDS

ROUGH DIAMONDS

40 ROOKIE
BRIAN BANNISTER
PITCHER

7 ROOKIE
ALEX GORDON
THIRD BASE

46 ROOKIE
JEREMY GUTHRIE
PITCHER

Kansas City Royals

- debuted with the New York Mets on April 5, 2006, and did not surrender a hit until the sixth inning
- joined the Royals in 2007 and finished his rookie season with a team-high 12 wins and a 3.87 ERA
- named AL Rookie of the Month in June and August 2007

40 ROOKIE
BRIAN BANNISTER
PITCHER

Kansas City Royals

- won the 2005 Golden Spikes Award as the best amateur baseball player in the US, and was drafted second overall by the Royals that year
- fast-tracked to majors after just one year in Double-A, where he had 29 home runs, 101 RBIs and a 1.015 OPS in 2006
- finished 2007 with 36 doubles, four triples and 15 homers to set a club record for extra-base hits by a rookie

7 ROOKIE
ALEX GORDON
THIRD BASE

Baltimore Orioles

- drafted in the first round by the Cleveland Indians in 2002 during a standout college career at Stanford
- made 15 bullpen appearances with Cleveland before being cast off and picked up by the O's
- started 26 games for the Orioles in 2007, going 7–5 with a 3.70 ERA

46 ROOKIE
JEREMY GUTHRIE
PITCHER

ROOKIE

DUSTIN PEDROIA
SECOND BASE

HOWIE KENDRICK
SECOND BASE

ROOKIE

DELMON YOUNG
OUTFIELD

Los Angeles Angels

- batted over .360 in four straight minor-league seasons (2003–2006)
- hit .303 after being recalled from Triple-A in 2006, finishing his first season with a .285 average
- battled two broken fingers (one in April, another in July) during his sophomore season and still batted .322

Boston Red Sox

- won AL Rookie of the Year in 2007 after batting .317, the best mark ever by a rookie second baseman
- struck out just 42 times in 581 plate appearances, the second-best ratio in the league
- committed only six errors in 137 games at second base

Minnesota Twins

- drafted first overall by the D-Rays in 2003
- made his debut in August 2006, weeks before his 20th birthday, and hit .317 in 30 games
- batted .288 with 13 home runs and 93 RBIs as a rookie in 2007

HOWIE KENDRICK
SECOND BASE

ROOKIE

DUSTIN PEDROIA
SECOND BASE

ROOKIE

DELMON YOUNG
OUTFIELD

ROUGH DIAMONDS

ROOKIE
RYAN BRAUN
THIRD BASE

35 COLE HAMELS
PITCHER

55 RUSSELL MARTIN
CATCHER

Milwaukee Brewers

- called up on May 25, 2007, and played just 113 games, but still captured NL Rookie of the Year honors
- batted .324 with 34 homers and a rookie-record .634 slugging percentage in 451 at-bats
- won NL Player of the Month honors in August 2007 with a league-leading 11 homers and 74 total bases

8 ROOKIE
RYAN BRAUN
THIRD BASE

Philadelphia Phillies

- started 23 games in his rookie season (2006), winning nine and posting an ERA of 4.08
- became the Phillies' ace in 2007, leading the team in wins (15), ERA (3.39) and strikeouts (177)
- selected to the 2007 National League All-Star Team

35 COLE HAMELS
PITCHER

Los Angeles Dodgers

- called up in 2006 and won the starting job when the Dodgers went 71–43 with him behind the plate
- batted .293 with 19 home runs and 21 steals in 2007, setting a team record for stolen bases by a catcher
- won Silver Slugger, Gold Glove and was starting catcher on the NL All-Star Team in 2007

55 RUSSELL MARTIN
CATCHER

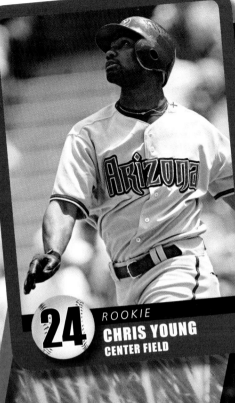

ROOKIE
24
CHRIS YOUNG
CENTER FIELD

2
ROOKIE
TROY TULOWITZKI
SHORTSTOP

11
RYAN ZIMMERMAN
THIRD BASE

Colorado Rockies

- batted .291 with 24 home runs while committing just 11 errors in his rookie season
- turned an unassisted triple play — the 13th in MLB history — on April 29, 2007
- broke Ernie Banks' NL record for home runs by a rookie shortstop when he hit number 20 on September 11, 2007

Arizona Diamondbacks

- drafted by the Chicago White Sox in 2001 and acquired by the D-Backs in 2005
- belted 32 home runs in his 2007 rookie season, including nine to lead off games, then added another leadoff homer in the NLDS
- stole 27 bases while being caught just six times

Washington Nationals

- runner-up for NL Rookie of the Year in 2006 after hitting 20 homers, driving in 110 runs, and leading the majors in hits with runners in scoring position
- followed up his debut by improving to 24 home runs in 2007
- had seven walk-off RBIs in 2006 and 2007 to the lead the majors

2
ROOKIE
TROY TULOWITZKI
SHORTSTOP

24
ROOKIE
CHRIS YOUNG
CENTER FIELD

11
RYAN ZIMMERMAN
THIRD BASE

20–20 club players who have collected 20 home runs and 20 stolen bases in the same season (*also* **30–30 club, 40–40 club**)

AL American League

ALCS American League Championship Series

ALDS American League Division Series

assist a throw by a fielder that results in a putout

Cactus League a schedule of exhibition games played in Arizona during spring training

call-up a minor-league player who is promoted to the major leagues in September, when the active roster expands from 25 to 40 players. Late-season call-ups are not eligible to play in the postseason

complete game a game in which the starting pitcher is not removed for a relief pitcher

cup of coffee a brief stint in the major leagues

cycle a single, double, triple and home run in the same game

disabled list a list of injured players who have been temporarily removed from the active roster in order to make room for a replacement. Players may be placed on either the 15-day or 60-day disabled lists and may not be activated until the end of that period

DL disabled list

DP double play

ERA earned run average

fielding percentage a statistical measure of a player's defensive ability, calculated by dividing assists and putouts by total chances

HBP hit by pitch

hold a statistical measure awarded to a relief pitcher who enters a game in a save situation (*see* **save**), records at least one out and exits without forfeiting the lead

junior loop the American League

K strikeout

loop league

Mendoza Line a .200 batting average, named for Mario Mendoza, a slick-fielding shortstop who batted .198 in 148 games in 1979

MLB Major League Baseball

NLCS National League Championship Series

NLDS National League Division Series

OBP on-base percentage

on-base percentage a statistic that measures the rate at which a hitter reaches base safely by getting a hit, drawing a walk or being hit by a pitch

OPS on-base plus slugging; a statistic that measures a hitter's overall performance by adding his on-base percentage and slugging percentage

park-adjusted ERA a statistical measure that factors in the ballpark when calculating ERA so as not to unfairly penalize pitchers who play in hitter-friendly stadiums

posting system a system agreed upon by Major League Baseball and Nippon Professional Baseball to provide Japanese teams with compensation when a player leaves to join a North American club. When a player under contract with a Japanese team asks to be posted, MLB teams may submit sealed bids. The team making the highest bid wins the exclusive right to negotiate with the player, and if the player signs with the MLB club, his former Japanese team receives the bid amount as compensation

putout a statistical measure credited to the defensive player who catches the ball to make an out, such as a batted ball caught on the fly or a throw caught by a infielder who records an out by stepping on a base or tagging a runner

quality start a game in which the starting pitcher lasts at least six innings and surrenders no more than three earned runs

RBI run batted in

roster the list of players who are eligible to play for a team. MLB clubs have a 25-man roster of active major-leaguers who dress for each game, and a 40-man roster that also includes minor-league players and those on the 15-day disabled list

Rule 5 draft an annual draft designed to prevent young players from languishing in the minor leagues. Players are eligible for the Rule 5 draft if they have not appeared on their club's 40-man roster within three or four years of signing. A team selecting a player in the draft must keep him in the major leagues throughout the next season

sacrifice hit a bunted ball that causes the batter to be put out at first base, but which advances a baserunner. Sacrifices hits do not count as an at-bat when calculating batting average

sacrifice fly a fly ball to the outfield that is caught for an out, but which allows a baserunner to score. A player hitting a sacrifice fly is credited with an RBI and the plate appearance does not count as an at-bat when calculating batting average

save a statistical measure awarded to a relief pitcher who enters a game when his team is ahead and completes it without relinquishing the lead. To be credited with a save, the pitcher must enter with a lead of no more than three runs and pitch at least one inning; or enter the game with the potential tying run either on base, at bat or on deck; or pitch at least three innings regardless of the score

senior loop the National League

Show the major leagues

slugging percentage a measure of a hitter's overall power, calculated by dividing total bases by at-bats

total bases a statistic that adds together the number of bases achieved through base hits (one for a single, two for a double, three for a triple, four for a home run)

total chances the number of plays in which a defensive player is involved. It is calculated by adding assists, putouts and errors

Triple Crown an informal term for the rare accomplishment of leading the league in three major categories. The hitters' Triple Crown consists of batting average, home runs and RBIs. For pitchers, the categories are wins, strikeouts and ERA

WHIP walks and hits per inning pitched

wild card a postseason berth given to the team with the best record among those that finished second in their division

GLOSSARY

ACKNOWLEDGMENTS

The author would like to acknowledge the following resources used during the research for this book: Baseball-Reference.com, JockBio.com, Retrosheet.org, *The Hardball Times, Baseball Prospectus, Sports Illustrated* (both in print and online at SI.com), and the network of MLB websites.

Special thanks to Steve Cameron, Barbara Campbell and Michael Worek at Firefly Books, as well as Jane McWhinney and Luna Design.

PROFILE INDEX